Secure Internet Practices

Best Practices for Securing Systems in the Internet and e-Business Age

Acknowledgments

Authors:
Patrick McBride
Jody Patilla
Craig Robinson
Peter Thermos

Contributors:
Jimmy Alderson
Bill Jaeger
Ed Moser
Steve Roberts
Tamara Savino
Erik Wolf

Editor:
Ed Moser

Illustrations:
Firstline Creative Resources, LLC
Charles Tomey
Erik Wolf

Reviewers:
Bob Austin
Chris Byrnes (META Group)
Matt Caston
Jeff Man
Robert Nesmith
Marc Othersen
Tamara D. Savino
Tom Scholtz (META Group)

Secure Internet Practices

Best Practices for Securing Systems in the Internet and e-Business Age

Patrick McBride
Jody Patilla
Craig Robinson
Peter Thermos
Edward P. Moser

AUERBACH PUBLICATIONS

A CRC Press Company

Boca Raton London New York Washington, D.C.

Library of Congress Cataloging-in-Publication Data

Catalog information may be obtained from the Library of Congress.

Co-published by

Auerbach Publications
(an imprint of CRC Press LLC)   and
2000 N.W. Corporate Blvd.
Boca Raton, FL 33431

METASeS
20464-A Chartwell Center Drive
Cornelius, NC 28031

Visit the Auerbach Publications Web site at www.auerbach-publications.com
Visit the METASeS Web site at www.metases.com

Table of Contents

Figures and Illustrations

Chapter 3: Web and e-Commerce Security

Appendix A: Sample Excerpt from an Information Security Program Gap Analysis

Appendix B: Excerpts from Technology Standards and Configuration Guides Publications

Appendix E: Trends in Security Spending

Preface

This report from METASeS is written for those who need to develop policies, programs, strategies, and tactics for dealing with the risks of Internet applications and e-Commerce. The intended audience is management from various levels who are involved in policy, financial, technical, and other decisions for achieving appropriate Internet security.

This book is not a detailed technical guide. It is an overview of security programs, policies, goals, life cycle development issues, infrastructures, and architectures aimed at enabling you to effectively implement security at your organization.

In addition to simply writing about general issues and solutions, we have attempted to give concrete examples where possible and to provide "templates" to expedite your own efforts in this exciting, rapidly changing arena.

Overview

The purpose of the report is to help an organization evaluate its Internet-related business risk, and create a workable security program, security policies, and architectures. This report is organized into the following chapters.

The **Introduction** provides an overview of the explosive growth of the Internet and its associated business applications, and the security implications of the e-Commerce revolution. A formula for quantifying risk is also presented.

Chapter 1 introduces our overarching security program. It discusses the issues organizations must consider when designing, developing, implementing, and operating security programs, including risk management. It also provides our Enterprise-Wide Security Program Model of a program's component parts.

This chapter also provides some practical advice on how to analyze an existing program, and best-practice recommendations for scoring "early wins" on tightening security in order to garner the institutional support for sustaining longer-term initiatives.

Chapter 2 covers a foundation stone of a security program – Information Security Policy. It describes the importance of policy, how to create it, and outlines its characteristics. The chapter also details the parts of the policy life cycle, describes standards and procedures, and outlines our Best-Practices Policy Framework. Given the importance of information policy in the Internet security space, and for security in general, this chapter spends considerable time on how to analyze, define, and improve current policies.

Indeed, in the first two chapters of the report, this book devotes much attention to program and policy before tackling architecture and infrastructure. After all, clear security policies and a sound security awareness program must exist to lay the foundation for effective protection of information.

Chapter 3 provides an overview of the fundamental security goals, architecture, and development methodology, including the system development life cycle. Moreover, it takes a detailed look at specific network infrastructure elements such as routers, servers, application issues, end-user issues, and security controls, and how they fit into the security architecture puzzle. For each element, this chapter provides a set of recommendations.

Note that chapter 3 discusses the technical details of Internet security. Chapters 1 and 2 outline many of the overarching security program elements that are independent of a given system or application, but are essential to establishing a secure environment. Chapter 3, however, drills down into the specifics of security.

The appendices provide specific examples and templates for security policies and standards, as well as list numerous other sources of invaluable information on Internet security.

Appendix A is a sample Information Security Gap Analysis.

Appendix B contains illustrative tables of contents and excerpts from two of METASeS' best practices technical publications, a UNIX Technology Standard and a Solaris Configuration Guide.

Appendix C contains links to important or interesting Web sites on Information Security.

Appendix D contains a comprehensive list of processes and procedures.

Appendix E contains excerpts on trends in security spending from the META Group report, Enterprise Security in Practice: Market Segments in Transition.

Research

This report represents a collective effort by many experts from METASeS. Representatives from our consulting practice and our applied research and development organization contributed to the development of the guide and its editorial review. In keeping with the company philosophy of crafting our intellectual capital into a form that is easily accessible by customers, this report attempts to condense and document as much of our collective Internet security wisdom as possible into a pragmatic set of best practices.

The primary source for the best practices in this report is our extensive consulting work with customers from various vertically integrated industries around the globe. Our clients include both U.S. and foreign governments, who are leveraging the Internet to provide more timely information to their constituents, and even running vast military communications networks over it. They include health care companies facing the daunting task of adopting this new medium while maintaining customer privacy, as well as meeting stringent regulatory requirements in the U.S. and Europe. Our collective experience extends to banking and financial services companies, where a mix of new Internet business applications and changing government rules are fundamentally altering the market.

Our client base encompasses the manufacturing sector, where competing corporations are leveraging the Internet to share supply chains and collaborate on research projects. Our work pertains to projects with telecommunications companies including global carriers, Internet Service Providers (ISPs), and cable and satellite companies. Our consulting work also includes projects for a host of "virtual" retailers and traditional brick and mortar organizations, in all, a tangled mix of organizations vying for customers in this new market frontier.

We further benefited from the use of our parent firm META Group's voluminous intellectual capital repository – representing 10 years of qualitative and quantitative research from more than 2,000 world-wide customers. Finally, our research included an exhaustive search into numerous publicly available sources of security information, which are referenced in Appendix C.

We owe a great debt to the numerous METASeS team members who generously contributed to this report and drew up a consistent set of concepts and best practices. We hope the report will help you to frame the Internet security problem, and provide a practical set of recommendations for improving your risk posture.

Terminology

One of the most difficult issues we faced in researching and developing this report was the extreme disparity in security terminology. The most daunting problem was the inconsistency in the definition and use of terms in security and risk management. While there are tomes written on the topic, many papers, reports, and studies we examined either used different terms to describe similar concepts, or used the same terms differently – even within the same text! So we spent a significant amount of time and effort overcoming terminology differences between our own team members. This was particularly true of security policy.

There are many different interpretations of "policy" from different organizations in various geographic locations and industry groups. The definitions for security policy range from top management directives to lower-level procedures and rules for such items as configuring firewalls. After considerable effort, we assembled a set of compatible definitions, which are in the Glossary.

The disparity in definitions was one of the major factors shaping the organization of this report. Lacking a commonly accepted set of public definitions for key security terms – even from the relevant U.S. government agencies – we believed it vital to offer up our own security vernacular. We don't expect this report to become the authoritative, universally accepted reference for security terms. However, providing a set of our definitions for key security concepts should make it much more useful and understandable. Sections 1 and 2, therefore, develop a set of terms and common models to serve as the framework for articulating our Internet security best practices.

Before beginning the report itself, we'd like to share a word on that loaded term – "best practices." As we in the consulting profession travel the globe to work with various organizations, we run into one little problem again and again. It seems that many in the senior and mid-level management ranks have been ordered to compare what they are doing against "industry best practice." While benchmark comparisons are noble undertakings, and we firmly believe that significant value can be derived from them in the right context, a few underlying assumptions about them need clarification.

The first assumption is that a "catalog" or "database" of industry best practices exists at all. In some cases, well-worn practice areas have been developed, studied and cataloged into a quantifiable industry "best practice" database. (Examples are data center operations, LAN/desktop management on the information technology (IT) side, or automobile underwriting in the business field). In many cases, however, there is simply no industry-level data. If any does exist, the ability to normalize the information to make it really useful in a comparative exercise is dubious.

The second underlying assumption is that if a particular practice is good, or "best" for an organization or for the industry as a whole, then it must be good for all organizations. The truth is some practices that work in one place or even within one industry would not be at all appropriate for your particular organization. Two of the most common and compelling reasons for this are differences in culture and business strategy.

Culture is one of the most difficult things to change within a company or government agency. Because it is such a powerful force, many would-be "best practices" need to be tested for their "cultural fitness" within your organization. Moreover, some firms, even within the same vertical industry, have wildly different strategies. Notable examples are traditional brick-and-mortar banks versus upstart Web-based banks or mortgage companies. What is best for one company, or for traditional business strategies in a particular industry, may not apply to another organization with a different agenda.

Any given field, including security, has a definitive set of generally acceptable practices that are useful when tailored to an organization's unique business needs. In this report, we will share the security-related ones with you, as well as some of our very own "best practices." There is not yet a definitive source of this information for the security field (we hope, in time, to create it.) Thus, these practices stem from our own experiences and those of the META Group Analyst teams gleaned from many years of work with customers world-wide. However, especially in the security field, it is more critical to understand what is truly "best" for your particular organization in the context of key factors such as your culture, business goals, return on investment (ROI) expectations, and risk tolerance. Some of these practices will be suitable to you, while others will not. While best practices can be truly useful, you need to tailor them to your organization.

Introduction

With the astonishingly rapid adoption of network computing and its e-Commerce derivatives, many businesses and government organizations have discovered in recent years that their security programs have serious deficiencies, including underfunding, especially relative to vastly increased risks. Most organizations have a very tight security budget. Because of the "overhead" nature of security, and the fact that it is often perceived as a "luxury," the appropriation of funds for informatation security purposes is often a struggle. Moreover, the Internet explosion caught organizations' IT departments, especially their security teams, by surprise. The proliferation of networks, Web servers and e-Commerce technologies throughout the business world has exacerbated the relative dearth of effective security measures.

Brief History of the Internet

By any measure, the Internet is a phenomenon that is transforming the way we communicate in our business and personal lives. Today the source of exploding online business between commercial firms and customers, the Internet had its roots in the defense sector. It originated in 1969 with ARPANET, an initiative of the Defense Department's Advanced Research Project Agency. It developed into a means for universities and research institutes to swap information and conduct research. By its first decade of operation, the Internet was enabling many of the functions we now associate with it: e-mail, file transfers, access of remote databases, and online discussions. The scientific community was vital in the Internet's formative years. In 1986, the National Science Foundation began NSFNET to link five research supercomputer installations, and inherited the Defense Department's ARPANET, thus forming the major "backbone" of high-speed Internet communication links.

As the Web site www.tui.edu/Help/History.html documents, a series of technical innovations and new user applications have spurred development and ease of Internet use. In 1973, the File Transfer Protocol (FTP) allowed users to receive files from remote computers. By 1982, a standard set of protocols, the Transmission Control Protocol and Internet Protocol (TCP/IP), permitted networked computers to converse in the same language. The use of TCP/IP as the standard Internet protocol has had important implications for security. TCP/IP, an open protocol that is independent of particular hardware and software vendors, has no authentication nor encryption, and almost no validation. Although it is highly flexible, it is especially open to attack.

Technical progress – and security risks – continued apace. In 1984, Apple introduced its Macintosh personal computer with a graphical user interface (GUI). The same year, science fiction writer William Gibson employed the terms "cyberspace" and "hackers" in his novel *Neuromancer*. In 1988, 22-year-old Cornell University student Robert Tappan Morris unleashed a worm program that crashed six percent of the Internet's servers. In 1989, Tim Berners-Lee devised the concept of the World Wide Web at the European Organization for Nuclear Research (CERN). The following year saw the introduction of hypertext markup language (HTML), and graphics were introduced onto Web pages in 1992. Marc Andreesen's creation of Netscape Navigator in 1994 permitted novice users to browse the Web with relative ease. Andreesen had been one of the designers of Mosaic, the first graphical browser, a prime example of the "freeware" that was to fuel the Web. And throughout the past 15 years, the widespread adoption of personal computers in the home and office helped spark widespread Internet use. And vice-versa: In 1999, use of home PCs jumped an astounding 41 percent, with much of the increase attributable to greater Internet use, according to Knight Ridder/Tribune Business News.

By 1995, Web pages were being widely used for the display of corporate advertisements and product information. Online magazines and other publications also became prevalent. Major news organizations such as CNN began setting up Web-based news sites in 1996. By 1997, individuals were increasingly building their own "home pages," and "netcasts" were transmitting audio programs through the Internet.

Size and Growth of the Internet

The growth of the Internet has been so rapid that it should soon constitute the largest single commercial marketplace on earth. It is remarkable to recall that in 1971 ARPANET had a grand total of 23 sites. Yet by 1997, the Internet encompassed over two million computers. Perhaps more remarkably, until about 1990, the Internet was, by policy and custom, off limits to commercial users! Modem speeds, which in 1983 were 1,200 bits per second (BPS), today operate at 56,000 (56K) bits per second, and are yielding to other ever-faster technologies like Digital Signal Lines (DSL), operating at more than 1 million bits per second.

In 1998, the estimated number of worldwide Internet users was 142 million, with 44 percent of these in the United States. That year, 63 million Americans used the Web; 171 million will by 2003. World-wide users are expected to exceed 500 million during 2000. The number of commercial email messages sent daily in the United States alone is estimated at 7.3 billion. The number of Web pages approximates 1 billion.

The bar chart in Figure i-1 illustrates the explosive past and projected future growth in the number of Internet users worldwide. Figure i-2 shows the rapidly rising number of Americans surfing the Internet.

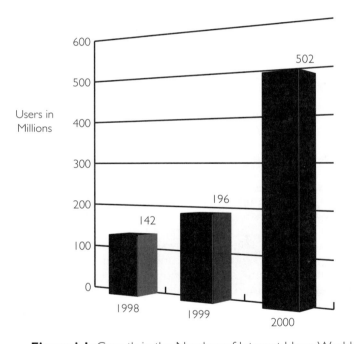

Figure i-1: Growth in the Number of Internet Users Worldwide

The recent growth of commerce on the Internet has been astronomical. According to the Center for Research in Electronic Commerce, the total Internet Economy grew 68 percent from the first quarter of 1998 to the first quarter of 1999. E-Commerce alone rose 127 percent during this period.

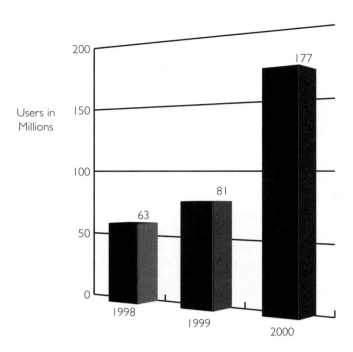

Figure i-2: Number of Americans Who Use the Internet

***NOTE:** "E-Commerce," often called "e-Business," may be defined as the use of the Internet, extranets, intranets, and corporate Web sites to supplement or replace traditional marketing, sales, and distribution outlets and methods.*

Online retail sales, which were $3 billion in 1997, are projected to exceed $40 billion in 2002, according to the META Group report *Electronic Commerce*. The increase of other services such as ticketing and financial services is equally rapid. Online trading alone is projected to grow from $11 billion in 1996 to a stunning $500 billion in 2000, according to Management Review. Total spending on e-Commerce was $50 billion in 1998, and will climb to $1.3 trillion in 2003, reported International Data Corporation. In the same period, business-to-business sales will rise from $131 billion to $1.5 trillion. The results for individual enterprises have been astonishing. For example, eBay, the online trading site, has swiftly built a vast, worldwide enterprise from the electronic selling of collectibles that had previously been relegated to flea markets, yard sales, and classified ads.

Figure i-3 illustrates the almost logarithmic growth of e-Commerce revenues in recent years.

One great advantage of the Internet, for consumers shopping for the products and services, is the ability to readily conduct extensive online research and make price comparisons. The seven most common products bought by Web customers are books, software, music, travel services, hardware, clothes, and electronic products.

Mergers and acquisitions (M&As) are a good measure of how an economy values an industry. According to Thomson Financial Securities, Internet-related mergers and acquisitions for the first half of 1999 totaled $43 billion, a rise of 63 percent over 1998.

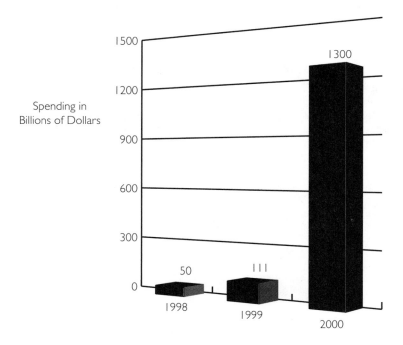

Figure i-3: Projected Growth of e-Commerce Revenues

Implications for Security

In such a huge market, the need for security measures, although making up only a fraction of total expenditures, will inevitably be significant. Revenues for Internet security worldwide are projected to rise from $3.1 billion in 1998 to $7.4 billion in 2000, doubling in just two years. In the market for firewalls alone, according to InfoTech Trends, expenditures are slated to increase to $1 billion in 2000 from $312 million in 1997, a rise of 100 percent per annum over three years. Over the next few years, information security is expected to be one of the seven areas of greatest employment need, right along with Internet development. Appendix E contains excerpts from a META Group report on trends in security spending, *Enterprise Security in Practice, Market Segments in Transition*.

Business Uses of the Internet

Businesses are rushing to incorporate the Internet into their operations because it enhances the efficiency and lowers the cost of so many commercial endeavors, while opening up myriad new opportunities.

Common Uses

Some of the most common current and future business uses of the Internet technologies are listed as follows:

- Electronic documents to slash publishing and paper costs
- Intranets to increase availability of corporate information to employees
- Web publishing to disseminate data or encourage interactive exchange of information between firms and customers
- Customer self-service
- Enhanced inventory management
- Supply chain management and manufacturer-supplier collaboration
- Electronic checking services
- Generation of customer data
- Online selling to cut costs, ease customer use, and expand around-the-clock services
- Less expensive service by cutting out the middleman; enhanced revenues by adding "reintermediators" who generate value-added applications
- Service chain management for proactive customer service
- Free access of corporate data and tools by customers, clients, and field service representatives
- Public posting of regulatory information and services by governments and large corporations

These uses are detailed in the following section.

Examples of Business Applications and Benefits

The Internet reduces administrative costs by converting paper documents to electronic media. Yet, contrary to predictions, we are nowhere near the "paperless office," as there is more intriguing information available to print than ever before. Almost all large companies now have an Intranet. The Web greatly enhances the access of employees to internal company information, and slashes publishing and distribution costs for the distribution of phone lists, human resource policies, and computerized data.

Businesses are using Web publishing to transmit an array of information types – sales information, corporate news, investor data, etc. Web publishing has a variety of modes that are becoming increasingly complex. The simplest form is static publishing, in which Web pages display information that seldom changes. In active publishing, the Web pages are updated regularly. In customized or personalized online publishing, users can choose the components of their Web sites, MyYahoo being a prominent example. In Web publishing that uses push technology, the accent is on interactive exchanges of data: email, pagers, handheld computers, and cell phones.

The Internet can dramatically improve inventory, procurement, and logistical controls. One of its greatest impacts is on supply chain management. Inefficient inventory management can lead to the oversupply of components, boosting inventory costs. Being out of stock can mean lost sales. But the instant communication of the Internet makes for far more efficient "just in time" inventory management. Procurement is eased by putting information online. Dell Computer, for instance, surged to the head of its sector through the rapid assembly and shipment of PCs procured through the Web.

Improved inventory management goes beyond greater efficiencies to foster actual collaborations among manufacturers and suppliers. For example, footware manufacturer Wolverine uses the Internet to collect and exchange purchase order and product spec data with factories, licensees, and customers.

The Internet also permits shifting customer service to self-service. Consumers can get the information they want more quickly than by dealing with a representative over the phone. While customers now have to spend time filling out online forms, they save even more time by not having to wait for forms to arrive in the mail. At the same time, labor and communications expenses for business are slashed. According to a major mutual fund, it costs $5-15 for every phone call to change the address on an account, but less than $1 if the customer does it over the Web.

For banks, a potentially vast Internet enterprise will be the use of electronic checks, or e-checks, over open networks. E-checks will reduce check processing costs by a factor of 5 to 10 and allow banks to add other online services to customers. Banks and many other businesses, Scotia Bank and Wells Fargo are examples, are also moving to offer certificate authority (CA) services using public key infrastructures (PKIs)[1] to enable trustworthy business-to-business commerce.

For organizations– such as banks, music companies, or publishing houses – in the business of providing and managing information, the Internet can generate new revenues through improved marketing and customer management. Such operations may produce more information about customers than anything previously available. This data can then be leveraged to create new products and services and build tighter relationships with customers. Thus, information about transactions may be more valuable than the transactions themselves.

Some companies such as Amazon.com sell exclusively online, while others, such as Charles Schwab, are shifting more of their transactions to an online mode. Secondary mortgage brokers such as Fannie Mae and Freddie Mac have moved to accepting and fulfilling electronic mortgage requests and delivering other services – for example, Web-based ordering and tracking of home inspections – to its primary lending partners. Online sales are far cheaper than traditional sales, as the Internet dispenses with the need for expensive, proprietary sales networks. The costs of business-to-business transactions are greatly reduced. Sales orders may be processed 24-7, independent of a sales force working 9 to 5. Processing of the orders themselves can be automated.

"Disintermediation" – cutting out the middleman, that is, brokers, retailers, agents, and sales personnel – is the short-term result of the corporate rush to foster direct electronic connections to its customer base. And in the middle- and long-term, "reintermediation" will occur in many industries as companies provide value-added services and broker business between buyers and sellers. Indeed, the major Internet portals, such as Yahoo and AOL, are reintermediators in the sense that their main "product" is access to people and assorted information, rather than any of their own corporate information. In short, they integrate and mediate access to external sources of data. Another example is Australia's

---

[1] PKIs consist of the policies, management, structure, and technology necessary for generating, distributing, and managing trusted digital certificates.

Legalco Online, which brokers access to online, publicly available information for such clients as lawyers and mortgage officers. Further, as companies like Amazon and eBay have branched out from selling books or holding auctions to offering a range of products and services, a discernible trend is the growth of e-Commerce "keiretsu," collections of online businesses offering a full suite of complementary services.

Effective service organizations such as banks and health care companies are starting to develop proactive approaches to customer service, performing rapid problem solving at the earliest point in support. Such companies are moving toward a "service chain" architecture that will integrate electronic process interchange (EPI) technology with document management, knowledge management, and customer information systems.

All users within and outside the organization – customers, customer service reps, field service technicians, etc. – will share documents and tools to enable better service and speed resolution of client problems. Customer service personnel will freely access corporate tools and data from remote client sites, and customers will freely access troubleshooting tools and reference materials to solve problems and to answer questions themselves.

One seeming countertrend to the growth of Internet applications will be the adoption of physical infrastructure by companies that have heretofore been exclusively "dot.com" enterprises. Until quite recently, Web-based businesses such as E-Trade and Drugstore.com minimized costs by avoiding such "brick and mortar" facilities as warehouses. However, the shipment of most goods will continue to require physical production, storage, and distribution. Therefore, the acquisition or building of real-world infrastructure will be a competitive asset for the "New Economy's" major players.

Government Uses

The Internet entails great cost efficiencies for large corporations especially governments, given their intense paperwork and public notification requirements. (Governmental Internet applications are often called electronic service delivery (ESD) to distinguish them from their more profit-oriented e-Commerce counterparts.) RFPs, proposals, public data, and negotiations flow much more quickly through networks than through traditional paper- and human-intensive procurement and communications channels. It can be daunting for a user to locate the correct office, form, or official in a large bureaucracy, but the Web offers the prospect of single-point-of-contact and one-stop-shopping. Among the services that governments are providing, through applications such as forms management and electronic data interchange (EDI), are the ability to:

- Browse regulations and legislation.
- Conduct online inquiries through Web-based "kiosks."
- Perform online purchasing.
- Apply for licenses and permits.
- Pay fees.
- File tax returns.
- Transmit tax payments or refunds.

Categories of e-Commerce

Given the vast assortment of businesses moving onto the Internet, it is useful to try to categorize e-Commerce. E-Commerce can be broken down in one of two ways, with one approach focusing on who the customer is, and the other stressing the relationship between seller and buyer.

In one respect, e-Commerce can be divided into: 1) Retail commerce; and 2) Business-to-business commerce. Retail commerce involves a business that sells directly to customers. An example is Amazon.com, which supplies digital markets for books and CDs, and has expanded into online auctions, toys, banking, and much else. Business-to-business commerce entails the sale of goods or services between commercial enterprises.

E-Commerce may also be divided into: 1) Customer relationship management (CRM); and 2) Supply chain management. Management of customer relations pertains to such areas as sales, marketing, and customer service, including presale and post-sale support. Supply chain management, for either manufacturing or services, involves the world of relationships between the providers of goods or services, their suppliers, and customers. In CRM, transactions take place in a continuum of pre-sale activities, sale transactions, and post-sale actions, the latter including shipping and customer service and support. In supply chain management, an example enterprise is Dell, which assembles its computers from a great many hardware and software vendors, based on specific orders placed by its customer base.

Security in the Internet and e-Commerce Age

In the past 30 years, the Internet has grown from a useful tool for academic research into an increasingly dominant platform for the conduct of business transactions. As the commercial stakes of the Internet have exploded, so have its risks. Connecting to the Internet is the physical security equivalent of placing an organization's front door on every browser in the world. And many organizations have numerous vulnerable "back doors" that end users may inadvertently open to intruders. Further, network administrators charged with guaranteeing the security of the business are strapped for time and resources.

E-business is a mad scramble – the 21st century equivalent of a California gold rush. The breakneck pace of e-Commerce and the focus on time to market – in both mature brick-and-mortar companies and new "dot.com" players – is placing strains on even the best IT and internal security organizations. Most companies simply can't keep up with the new challenges.

The risk of a security breach is much greater today, and the consequences can be devastating. Risk is defined as the likelihood of loss, damage, or injury. Risk is present if a threat can exploit an actual vulnerability to adversely impact a valued asset. Figure i-4 lists the major Internet security threats reported by companies.

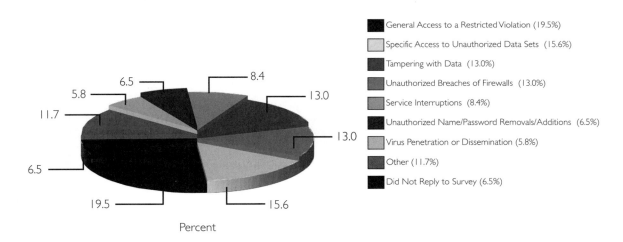

Figure i-4: Major Internet Security Threats Reported by Companies

A Formula for Quantifying Risk

Fortunately, you need not be defenseless against security vulnerabilities. The security risk for your organization can be quantified and compared to other organizations, and can help you start to plot out your security plan. Refer to the formula in Figure i-5.

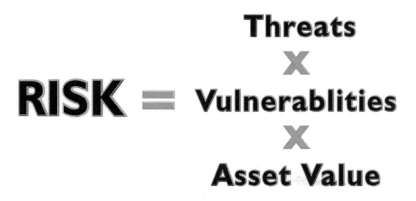

Figure i-5: A Risk Equation

In the equation, *threats* refers to crackers[2] or others who could try to break into your network – from without or within – and compromise your data. They also include people or things that may purposefully, inadvertently, or accidentally harm assets. Internal employees, for example, may accidentally damage or destroy valuable information. Vulnerabilities mean the holes or weaknesses in information systems and procedures that intruders can exploit. Asset value means the worth of the data that intruders target.

Security Challenges

For each aspect of the equation, any organization connected to the Internet or engaged in e-Business faces significant challenges.

Information Value

First, the value of the information transmitted over and accessible via the public Internet and e-Commerce, and thus its attendant risk, is exploding. Moreover, an organization's corporate assets (its intellectual capital, business plans, financial assets, etc.) are increasingly stored in systems connected to a very public Web. The Internet also increasingly exposes client data to unauthorized disclosure. Whether organizations are engaged in retail or business-to-business e-Commerce, their customers – aware of these risks – are demanding the safeguarding of their personal and business information.

To date, much of the press attention on Internet security has focused on information in transit – for example, the pilfering of credit card numbers or passwords as they traverse

---

[2] We use the term "cracker" to refer to someone who illicitly and electronically tries to break into a system. Technically, a "hacker" can refer to someone who is authorized to break into a system, often to test the system's vulnerabilities.

networks. In truth, however, stealing data in transit is "chump change," the cyber equivalent of purse snatching. Years ago, when famed bank robber Willie Sutton was asked why he robbed banks, he replied, "Because that is where the money is." In the 21st century, Willie's equivalent statement is, "Crackers will break into internal corporate networks because that is where the money is."

A Rising Threat

Second, the threat is increasing. There are significantly more efforts to try to break into company networks than ever before. Worldwide, viruses penetrated about 64 percent of firms, according to the 1999 Information Week Research Global Information Security Survey. A year ago, about half of firms surveyed reported no system downtime due to security breaches. This year, only 36 percent could make that claim. The threat ranges from novice cyber vandals looking to deface public Web sites, to unsavory IT insiders seeking to steal valuable corporate information, to very knowledgeable cyber espionage agents with sophisticated attack methods looking to lift critical corporate assets for personal or political gain.

Figure i-6 shows the steady rise in security breaches reported by corporations, universities, and government agencies.

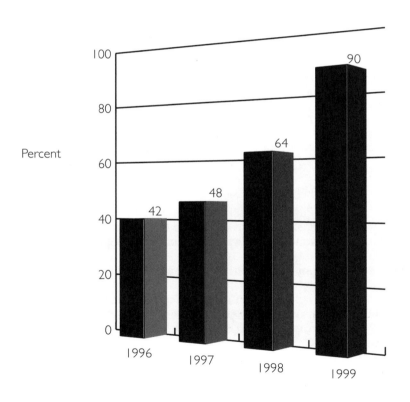

Figure i-6: Percentage of Security Breaches Reported by Organizations

Companies are responding to the growing threat by, among other things, purchasing more security software and hardware applications. Use of virtual private networks for secure data transmission rose to 27 percent in the year 2000 from 11 percent a year earlier. From 1997 to 1998, according to ICD, the market for firewalls rose 80 percent, encryption software 31 percent, and anti-virus software 28 percent. Revenues for security authentication, authorization, and administration increased 46 percent.

Figure i-7 illustrates the rapid growth in Internet security revenues.

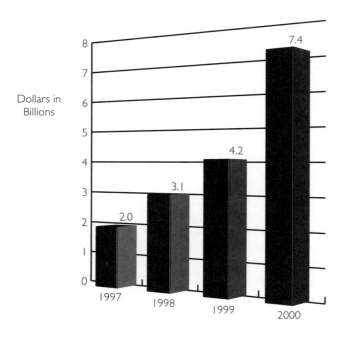

Figure i-7: Growth in Internet Security Revenues

Historically, most threats occurred within an organization. While current studies show insiders still constitute a larger hazard, the ratio has significantly changed in the last several years. Just two years ago, the proportion of internal versus external security breaches was 70 to 30. Figure i-8 illustrates the current proportion of internal versus external security breaches: 58.4 percent of violations are internal, and 41.6 percent are external, according to META Group. The ratio is moving toward a 50-50 split.

The Danger from Technological Change
Third, companies are exposed to an array of new vulnerabilities. A pressing issue is that hardware, software and application vendors who provide the "raw materials" for e-Commerce systems are hostage to time-to-market demands, just like the developers building the Web and e-Commerce applications. These vendors are churning out new products and product versions at an increasingly rapid clip, often without designing or testing them to guarantee they are secure. Indeed, applications are often designed purely with the business end in mind, while security needs are ignored or given short shrift. E-business applications are being cobbled together from a plethora of often-immature technologies whose very novelty makes them risky.

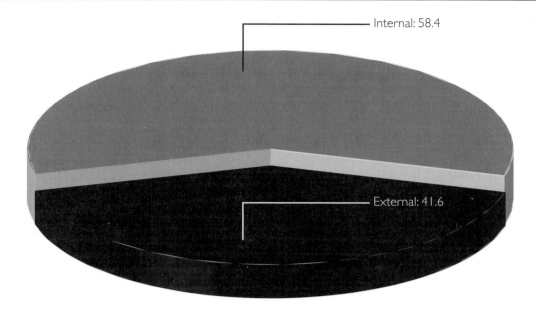

Internal: 58.4

External: 41.6

Figure i-8: Proportion of Reported Security Breaches: Internal vs. External

Applications developed at such speeds frequently contain "holes," inherent vulnerabilities that crackers can exploit. Alternatively, their design may be relatively secure, but application developers may have neither the time nor resources to test security or to fully implement security features.

Moreover, when hardware and software components and applications are installed, they are often poorly configured. A password system may be set up, for example, with default settings that would be the first thing crackers examine in trying to break into the system. Or an email system might be put in place without installing an anti-virus utility.

An important source of vulnerabilities is the lack of security expertise in most companies. The META Group report *Enterprise Security in Practice* estimated that fully 93 percent of organizations have unmet security needs. In personnel terms, this inadequacy is often a matter of demand outrunning supply. Security specialists may simply not be available, or even knowledgeable security personnel may be performing security functions on a part-time basis. Security technicians may be familiar with general network issues, but may not have received IT training in the many new areas of Internet-related network security. Corporate attempts to gain proficiency in Internet security are complicated by the difficulty of keeping pace with the breakneck technological change, and by the sheer number of vendors flooding the market with security products.

When security personnel may have an inadequate grasp of Internet security, employees in other departments are likely to have even less expertise. Lack of end-user awareness about standard security practices is a critical vulnerability. End users who do not receive basic security training might commit rudimentary errors such as inadvertently giving out sensitive information by phone. "Social engineering" is a common cracker ploy that targets naive users. In these situations, crackers telephone unsuspecting workers while posing as network administrators or other legitimate technicians. They might request the users' passwords and user IDs, or other information useful for compromising systems, all as part of a "system test" of security!

The number and volume of security breaches caused by external attackers is increasing. Such breaches include computer viruses, destructive "worms" that can replicate themselves, "Trojan horses", and Denial of Service attacks, like buffer overflows that overwhelm a process's ability to handle data.

Growing Consequences of Security Breaches

The asset value of the data and information assets and products that are vulnerable can be considerable. The consequences of a security breach include the following areas:

Denial of Service (DoS), Revenues, and Products – A cracker's intrusion into a Web site can result in Denial of Service (DoS), making the site inoperable. If the site serves as the "store front" for the business, the intrusion can cripple the entire business for the duration of the security breach. Results of a DoS attack can be wide-ranging and long-lasting. The immediate consequence is loss of current revenues. However, there is often a future revenue loss due to frustrated customers who migrate to another online option. For example, a book purchaser, if stymied in accessing or using Amazon.com, might frequent Barnes&Noble.com. Even worse, DoS can mean a severe loss to brand name, as the intrusion damages a firm's reputation as a reliable vendor.

Loss of Privacy – A cracker entering a database containing sensitive customer information can shatter the trust of customers about the confidentiality of their personal information. The more sensitive the data in question, the worse the fallout from a security breach. Severe consequences would result, for example, from the penetration of credit card or medical databases.
Privacy issues are of particular importance with governmental Internet services because so much government data – tax records, vehicle registration forms, Social Security checks – is thought to be confidential.

Legal Liability – Given the interconnectedness of enterprises in the Internet world, a cracker will at times access one firm in order to access other firms. In such an event, the first company in question is potentially liable for losses incurred by the other companies that are penetrated later. These breaches typically occur in supply chains where firms are "upstream" or "downstream" from the first company targeted.

Not only is the risk of being compromised greater today, but the consequences from a breach are potentially much more devastating. On one end of the spectrum, the results of a breach are direct financial losses. For example, if a cracker takes down a Web ordering system with a DoS attack, direct monetary losses, while bad enough, are simply equivalent to the number of hours the system was down multiplied by the revenue or profit per hour of the system. On the other end of the spectrum, the consequences of a breach are much wider and longer-lasting. For example, if a cracker gains access to the credit card database or other personal customer information, the impact can be loss of brand equity, customer confidence, and a potentially devastating loss of corporate value.

Indeed, the results of a security breach in today's interconnected world, combined with the swift reaction of the press corps hungry for news about the Internet, can deal your company a body blow. Consider the consequences of a cracker breaking into your public Web site to spread profane prose and illicit pictures. This is akin to airing negative TV commercials about your own company. Imagine what a negative, 30-second spot on the evening news about the breach would do to your corporate image. Such negative publicity can shred perceptions about product brands that took many years and significant investments to create. Most organizations would pay dearly to recover from this kind of incident.

The possible results of industrial espionage are also very sobering. The Internet can literally serve as a network rail car carrying away vast amounts of your organization's intellectual property. In fact, respondents to a Computer Crime and Security survey who could quantify computer-crime-related financial losses indicated their total losses averaged $120 million per year from 1997 to 1999 (Figure i-9). The damages were just the tip of the iceberg, as they represented only "reported" losses.

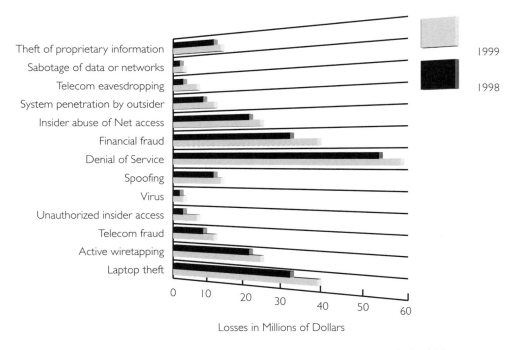

Figure i-9: Percentage Breakdown of Computer Crimes, 1998-1999

These issues and new risks are not confined to the private sector. Governmental organizations the world over are suffering the same invasions to their Web sites. In May 1999, the U.S. Department of Commerce, the U.S Department of Energy, and even the White House were hit by crackers.

Perhaps the best illustration of how EVERYONE is vulnerable to attack in the new Internet world was a cracker's successful penetration of the White House Web site.

A text portion of the cracker's Web page follows. The sample has been edited, given the foul language the cracker employed:

> *"Look at the interesting things we found in Bill's personal files.*
> *Why did we hack this domain? Simple, we could.*
> *Maybe this will teach the world a lesson. Stop all the*
> *war. Consintrate [sic] on your own problems. Nothing was*
> *damaged, but we not telling how we got in. Fear the end of*
> *the world is upon us, in a few short months it will all be over.*
> *Following peeps get some shouts:*
> *gH World Domination*
> *Fjear. wuz here [sic]."*

The following is an excerpt of an actual interview between a reporter and the White House cracker, alias "John Smith." It speaks volumes about the need to upgrade security, from the corporate board room to the presidential suite:

Reporter - "Why the particular attack on whitehouse.gov?"
John Smith - "Because it was easily exploitable...and was pretty high profile."
Reporter - "Were there any political reasons? Personal reasons?"
John Smith - "It wasn't specifically targeted for an attack, so it wasn't a political reason...As for personal reasons...it always feels good to get into a high profile place."

Conclusion

Far from being a passing novelty, the Internet is here to stay. It is fundamentally changing the way we do business and the way we conduct our lives. The Web's scope and rate of change are stunning, and are contributing to the vastly greater opportunities and risks facing business. Given the consequences of a security breach in the Internet age, organizations around the globe are struggling to bolster their network defenses. The solutions will not be simple.

Substantially improving an organization's security related risk posture requires a blend of strategic and tactical initiatives and a thorough, multi-year security improvement plan. Further, there is no single "silver bullet" technological fix – period! We believe that improving risk management and sustaining those improvements is a complex problem of many dimensions and requires security enhancements implemented in parallel.

The solution lies in developing a security program. A "program" is a high-level strategy that encompasses all the different elements your various personnel and business divisions need to do. A well-conceived, articulated, and executed program will eliminate many of the deep-seated, systemic security issues, and network- or Internet-related security issues in particular. Chapter 1, which follows, lays out METASeS' security program in detail. Chapter 2 discusses policy. A program and policy are the prerequisites — the building blocks, the *sine qua non* – of a solid security architecture and infrastructure, which are covered in chapter 3.

It is important to realize you do not have to wait two or three years to reap the rewards – that is, an improved risk posture – of implementing a security program. In fact, you can substantially reduce your organization's risk in three to six months, and this "early win" approach coupled with a philosophy of sustained improvement are key tenets of our strategy. Still, a complete program may take a few years to fully implement. The bottom line is that adequate security is not a destination – a place that you magically arrive in a short time. Rather it is a journey, an ongoing process, that involves constant enhancements and additions to your security practices, a challenge that can last for many years.

The Information Security Program 1

Some will find it surprising that, in this chapter, we do not discuss firewalls, perimeter security, vulnerability reduction, threat monitoring, operating system hardening, and all the other important technical components of an Information Security program. After all, this report is primarily about Internet security, and such security components are vital to that end. However, a great many of the organizations with whom we've worked have lacked something much more fundamental – an overall strategy to tie together those pieces and other critical elements. Our experience has been that organizations often undertake unconnected initiatives resulting in poor Internet security, or worse, a false sense of security. The disturbing refrain, "We have a firewall and so we are safe," is all too often repeated. Approaching Internet security with a fragmented set of initiatives almost guarantees an open door for crackers and other malicious intruders.

So, it is vital to craft a top-level strategy for mitigating your organization's exposure to security threats. Many factors are critical in this, but none is as important as a clear overall picture of important objectives. Documenting and explaining your main goals will help everyone in the organization follow the same risk reduction path.

As we explained in the preface, one of the toughest problems in crafting this report was agreeing on a common set of definitions. For you, too, a challenging task will be developing and communicating a common vocabulary and a common vision to personnel that may hail from diverse business and technical backgrounds. Your employees may already have their own concepts and terminology about what constitutes Information Security. A resulting communication breakdown among corporate divisions could block clear management articulation of Information Security strategy.

Another obstacle to enhanced security is that many people and their organizations do not take a "holistic" view of the problem. Few people have spent much time analyzing the overall security challenge and its attendant solutions. Their view often reflects and is constrained by organizational roles. Networking professionals, for example, typically look at the issue from the perspective of network technologies. Many employees, in part because of their occupational bias, only examine one or two narrow features of a security problem that in fact has many complicated aspects.

In an attempt to address such concerns, this chapter provides you with our overall "picture" of an Information Security program. METASeS calls this its Enterprise-Wide Information Security Program Model. The Enterprise-Wide Information Security Program Model defines and describes the high-level functions and components of an Information Security program.

The Enterprise-Wide Information Security Program Model is tailored to support business operations in both current and anticipated information systems environments. With the Enterprise-Wide Information Security Program Model as a guide, organizations can achieve these key goals:

- Establish their information risk management objectives.

- Identify the corporate information assets needing protection, and what they need to protect them against.

- Develop or refine the organization's Information Security policy, standards, procedures, and processes.

- Establish or refine the governance for Information Security.

- Build an enterprise security architecture.

- Define and build security infrastructure.

- Based on the security objectives, follow a life cycle approach to developing, implementing, and maintaining effective Information Security solutions.

The Present Information Systems Environment

The Information Revolution is transforming the commercial world. As outlined in the Introduction, this ongoing revolution is reflected by the exponential increase in Internet use, the heightened reliance on computer systems and networks to conduct business, and the rapid turnover in new computer technology. The environment for information systems has changed dramatically (Figure 1-1).

The potential risks resulting from this dynamic new picture present formidable challenges to Information Security professionals. As security concerns continue to branch out from the computer room to the boardroom, the stereotype of the "wild eyed," teenaged cracker no longer applies. The threat now ranges from the naive intrusions of untrained internal users to the sophisticated, focused attacks of well-funded external organizations, such as organized crime gangs or foreign espionage agencies. (These threats may increasingly target infrastructure. Telecommunication firms, banks, transportation networks, power and utility companies, oil and gas producers, and emergency services are all critical elements of national and regional infrastructures, and all rely heavily on distributed information systems. As a result, they are now on the front lines of the expanding cyber battleground.)

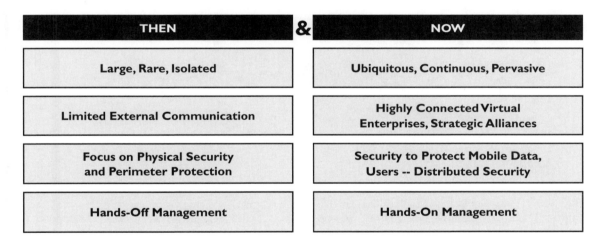

THEN	&	NOW
Large, Rare, Isolated		Ubiquitous, Continuous, Pervasive
Limited External Communication		Highly Connected Virtual Enterprises, Strategic Alliances
Focus on Physical Security and Perimeter Protection		Security to Protect Mobile Data, Users -- Distributed Security
Hands-Off Management		Hands-On Management

Figure 1-1: Changes Over Time in the Characteristics of Information Systems

A Risk Construct

A useful tool for designing an information security program is a "risk construct." A risk construct visually illustrates the layers of threats faced by an organization. The risk construct extends well beyond the top-level operations arena where business activities are conducted. As shown in Figure 1-2, business operations are layered atop networks that in turn are supported by systems and components.

Figure 1-2: Information System's Layered Zone of Risk -- Operations, Networks, Systems, & Components

The resulting zone of risk is widespread and diverse, and increasingly subject to penetration by knowledgeable crackers as well as by less technically astute intruders as "hacker tool kits" proliferate.

These tool kits contain modified programs that function exactly the same as the original programs, but allow the intruder to be "invisible" on the system. For example, the "login" program can be modified to let the intruder gain privileged access when specific characters are entered in the login or password field. In addition, the program is modified to prevent system logging of the intruder's actions. Other tool kit programs include the "ls" command, which lists the files on a UNIX system and can be modified to hide files, and "ps," which shows the current running processes and can be modified to hide processes the intruder is running. Other modified commands create back doors into the system and hide intruder activity.

The avenues of unauthorized entry are many. An intruder might use a password cracking utility to employ automated tools to remotely probe for vulnerabilities on common network services such as Network Information Service (NIS), Network File System (NFS), File Transfer Protocol (FTP), and Trivial File Transfer Protocol (TFTP). Someone could also walk into an organization, perform dialup access, and use a remote network administration application such as pcAnywhere. An attacker may gain access to business systems and impact business operations. Intruders can exploit the vulnerabilities found in system elements to attempt to penetrate other networks. Further, attacks may originate from within the organization. The situations above could apply equally to an internal employee, a contractor or, in a scenario increasingly common in e-Commerce, to external third parties granted access to certain internal resources.

Information Risk Management

Information risk management is the identification, assessment, and appropriate mitigation of vulnerabilities and threats that can adversely impact the organization's information or data assets. Organizations are increasingly using risk management to identify and reduce these information system risks in an efficient and cost-effective manner. Under risk management, operational considerations such as system performance and business concerns such as scheduling new product rollouts are addressed in tandem with security concerns. Balanced and traceable processes are employed. Such an approach generally yields an overall Information Security plan that encompasses both operational performance and system protection.

Your information risk management strategy should operate within several key parameters. A central precept is that risk – the chance of financial loss or damage to corporate products, data, or reputation – only exists if a threat has the potential to do real damage – to take advantage of an existing vulnerability, and go on to impact a valued asset. Another key concept is that it is generally impossible, from a cost or systems view and thus inappropriate, to totally eliminate information systems risk. An organization should prioritize the business operations and functions needing to be protected and perform a cost/benefit analysis to make an informed risk management decision on what to protect and to what degree.

In brief, an effective information risk management strategy requires you to perform actions such as the following:

- Identify key assets. You must know what you need to protect before trying to protect it.

- Ascertain and determine the importance of relevant vulnerabilities. The vulnerabilities will have different degrees of severity, impact, and likelihood of occurrence.

- Assess applicable threats. The threats also will vary according to severity, impact, and likely occurrence.

- Deploy cost-effective controls that best mitigate the risks. The appropriate solution might be to educate users, change administrative practices, or monitor for intrusion, etc.

- Periodically re-assess risk. The factors that made up the original risk decision need to be periodically reevaluated.

Enterprise-Wide Information Security Program Model: Functional Overview

The correct approach for formulating a proper security program is evolving. In the past, Information Security professionals typically competed with or ignored the business units in establishing Information Security. More recently, through the growing use of risk management strategies, companies have stressed an integrated development of security through the coordination of Information Security, business, customer service, and other operations.

The Enterprise-Wide Information Security Program Model provides the framework to develop, implement, and maintain integrated Information Security solutions that match your risk management objectives (see Figure 1-3).

Figure 1-3: The Enterprise-Wide Security Program Model

The Enterprise-Wide Information Security Program Model, as Figure 1-3 indicates, applies to processes throughout the security life cycle. The model's outer ring depicts key functions in the life cycle: assess, design, implement, and manage. The inner elements depict the core components of the security program: policies, standards, and procedures, processes, organization (governance), and technology.

Assess, Design, Implement, Manage

As the outer ring of the model illustrates, your organization should continuously perform the following functions:

1. Assess the security risks to business operations.

2. Design security solutions to appropriately address the assessed risks. (The solutions are the sum of policies, standards, and procedures, technology, process, and organization.)

3. Implement the appropriate security solutions.

4. Manage the overall security program and the constituent security solutions to assure their effectiveness.

Each function is discussed in detail in the sections that follow.

The organization can perform these functions directly, or outsource them and ensure they are implemented effectively. One of the imperatives of the security program model is to perform these functions continuously. Figure 1-3 depicts the idea, noted earlier, that the goal of security should be viewed as an ongoing process, not as a one-time destination.

Business, technology, and risk are not static. Your organization will undergo many new business or Information Technology initiatives that will force your security team to review the currency of the Enterprise-Wide Information Security Program Model. However, the Model, if properly implemented, will not itself change. The process of change is built into it, as the circular representation of its functions in Figure 1-3 shows.

When important business activities change, you should apply one or more of the four security functions anew. Such business activities would include, for example, the following:

- Launching of an important new business initiative
- Enhancement of business processes
- Initialization of mergers and acquisitions
- Changes to the Information Technology infrastructure (networks and systems)
- Opening of new offices, or moving the location of existing offices

Even if activities like the ones listed do not occur for a long time – however unlikely that possibility for most enterprises – organizations must periodically re-evaluate their security program relative to inevitable new vulnerabilities.

Assess Risks

Assuming that you are at the assessment phase of the life cycle, you start by determining the valuable information assets that your organization wishes to protect, and the threats and vulnerabilities to them. Often the weakest link is the lack of written policies, procedures, and standards on security or a lack of security awareness among the user community – particularly among administrators.

We recommend that, as part of the assessment function, Information Security organizations perform the following tasks:

- Work with business units to identify and prioritize business operations (for example, the billing process or the Web-based ordering system), thereby establishing how critical the various operations are.

- Establish specific objectives for business asset protection (for example, availability and privacy).

- Identify and assess high-level categories of vulnerabilities to the business information assets.

- Identify and evaluate the threats that can exploit the identified vulnerabilities.

- Determine the risk management metrics.

- Prioritize risks by analyzing the requirements for protecting individual business assets, as well as vulnerability and threat data.

- Prioritize the requirements for mitigating risk. You may not always mitigate a risk. However, you may manage it or decide it is worth the risk to do little or nothing about it.

Design Security Solutions

The next function in the life cycle is to design security solutions to appropriately address the assessed risks.

> **NOTE:** *Be aware that "solution" in this context refers to a suite of processes, procedures, training, hardware/software technical tools, etc. It does not only refer to the security technology elements. A solution is likely to entail several new processes, some new software, perhaps some new hardware, new monitoring of all of the above, and additional training. A "technological band-aid" is NOT a solution.*

Some of the steps that Information Security organizations might take are:

- Build Information Security road maps to guide development and integration of security solutions. These solutions should satisfy the risk mitigation requirements.

  Usually the solutions will be either strategic or tactical. A strategic solution attempts to deal with the systemic causes of the vulnerabilities in the information system. For example, a Web server hosting an e-Commerce site and deployed in the company's DMZ might be running in default mode, and thus be vulnerable. The tactical solution is to change the server's configuration and settings. The strategic solution is to fix the administration, change management, and deployment of Web servers that allow a vulnerable condition in the first place.

- Establish solution evaluation programs to demonstrate the operational effectiveness of the selected solutions. For example, identify metrics for measuring the effectiveness of solutions, such as how well users are adapting to new rules of behavior (for instance, having to change their passwords periodically).

- Develop specific technical controls, implementation plans and architectures, processes, and procedures that involve detailed technical representations of the solution. Determine the consequences for non-compliance and who is responsible for enforcement.

- Try to obtain a budget sufficient for your aims. Make some cost/benefit analyses of proposed solutions, then prioritize what can be implemented and how soon.

Modifying behaviors, incidentally, can make the budget you are allotted go further. It is typically a relatively inexpensive mitigation, compared to the purchase of new security systems. One of the best uses of the security program budget is security awareness "marketing." This would include traditional marketing activities like advertising (mailings, posters, giveaways, contests, etc.), as well as more formal training activities (such as in-service training, and new hire training). One of the most significant vulnerabilities to an organization is the human factor – "dumb" actions that employees, partners, contractors, and customers take, or fail to take, that put the organization's assets at risk. Thus, initiatives aimed at modifying behavior can provide a much larger return on investment (ROI) than any single tool or technology.

Implement Security Solutions

After assessing vulnerabilities and designing solutions for them, you put the solutions into effect. To do this, organizations can take some of the following steps:

- Obtain the procedural authority to implement specific solutions.

- Establish pilot programs for selected solutions. A solution should be carefully tested before it is put into widespread use to uncover problems and make refinements in a controlled environment.

- Provide necessary security awareness training throughout the organization prior to putting the solutions in practice.

- Pursue larger-scale solutions (typically implemented in bite-sized pieces) that follow the Information Security road maps.

Manage the Security Program

The final step is to manage the overall security program and the constituent security solutions. To accomplish this, some of the steps that we recommend Information Security organizations take are:

- Use established risk management criteria and metrics to monitor and measure the effectiveness of deployed solutions.

- Establish and maintain capabilities to respond to and recover from security incidents.

- Refine security objectives and the security solutions as operational experience is gained.

The Enterprise-Wide Information Security Program Elements: Framework, Organization, Technology, and Process

The security life cycle functions discussed above should help you improve your organization's security and maintain an acceptable risk posture over time.

Recall the elements listed in the interior of the Enterprise-Wide Information Security Program Model (refer to Figure 1-3). These are the component parts of a security program. They include:

- Information Security Policy Framework[1] Elements: Policies, Standards, and Procedures
- Organization
- Technology
- Process

Each is outlined in the sections that follow. Chapter 2 discusses the Information Security Policy Framework in detail, while chapter 3 covers Information Security technology and infrastructure. Appendix D has a listing of security and security-related processes.

Information Security Policy Framework

The Information Security Policy Framework – security policies, standards, and procedures – provides the overall foundation for an effective Information Security program. Figure 1-4 illustrates the hierarchical relationships between policies, standards and procedures found in an Information Security Policy Framework.

Organization, Technology, and Processes

The other elements of the Enterprise-Wide Information Security Program Model are: organization, technology, and processes.

Organization

The organization component of the Enterprise-Wide Information Security Program Model addresses the overall governance of the Information Security program. It covers organizational and employee infrastructure, including departments, reporting relationships, and key personnel, that will implement, maintain, and support the security program. The organization component extends beyond the designated Information Security staff. The IT organization, as well as end users, consultants, and outsourced help, play a critical role in supporting Information Security. In addition, the security organization component covers training and awareness programs for internal employees and external consultants, partners, and customers.

Technology

The technology component of the Enterprise-Wide Information Security Program Model addresses the technical tools required to implement and measure the program. These tools

---

[1] Framework is a collective term that refers to policies, standards, and procedures.

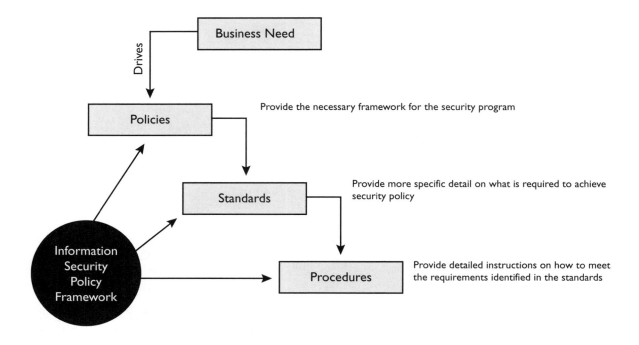

Figure 1-4: Policies, Standards, & Procedures -- A Hierarchical Framework for an Effective Security Program

include technical infrastructure, such as networks and systems, as well as specific security products like the following:

- Firewalls
- Enhanced authentication – Hard and soft tokens, digital certificates, biometrics, etc.
- Single sign-on or reduced sign-on
- Intrusion detection (network and host-based)
- Vulnerability scanning
- Antiviral software
- Encryption
- Virtual Private Networks (VPNs)
- Public Key Infrastructure (PKI)
- Directory services
- And many more

Processes

In the process component of the Enterprise-Wide Information Security Program Model, you address how to integrate the policies, standards, and procedures and the organization and technology components, and how to apply them to the security program. You must consider process improvements as your organization evolves and as you apply new technologies to the security infrastructure. You must keep processes up to speed with new business and new technologies. A well-known business equation (Figure 1-5) captures the requirements of failing to meet this requirement.

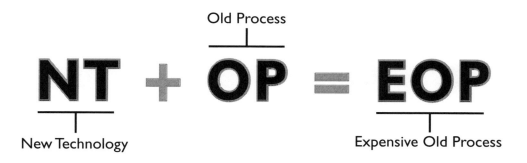

Figure 1-5: The Need to Keep Process Up-to-Date with Technology

Process refers to longer-term elements that might take days or weeks, or even be ongoing in nature. It should not be confused with procedures, which are shorter-term elements that typically last minutes, hours, or days. Figure 1-6 provides examples of both.

Process (Longer Running)	Procedure (Shorter Term)
IT Technology Review	How to Harden Windows NT, UNIX, etc.
Security Architecture Development	Intrusion Detection System Configuration
Security Program Development	Steps for Securing Logon
Risk Assessment	Threat or Vulnerability Analysis

Figure 1-6: Examples of Processes & Procedures

Appendix D provides many examples of common processes and procedures.
It is important to note that numerous processes, not directly controlled by the security organization, are key to the smooth operation of the security program. Some examples are:

- **Systems and Network Configuration and Change Management** – The process for executing and documenting changes or new features to various systems, networks, middleware, and applications. Policy and procedures should control this. Evaluate changes for their potential impact on the established overall risk posture.

- **Application Development Life Cycle** – The end-to-end process for building or buying an application, thus fulfilling business requirements, and then maintaining the application in accordance with changing requirements. Organizations are notorious for not building security into the product development life cycle. However, the spread of e-Commerce is forcing the issue onto many firms. (See the section System Development Life Cycle Methodology in chapter 3, as well as the METASeS publication *Secure Systems Development Life Cycle (SDLC)*.

- **IT Architecture** – The process for documenting and defining the current and future state of an organization's technology infrastructure and applications.

- **Systems/Network Management and Contingency Management** – The set of processes that keep an organization's infrastructure and applications running efficiently. These processes minimize the impact of adverse events and ensure an orderly restoration of the IT capability. (Note that security functions, particularly in the case of system performance, can impact system efficiency.)

- **Personnel Life Cycle** – The process of hiring, promoting, retiring, or dismissing employees, contractors, and consultants. For example, if an employee leaves, his system access privileges need to be promptly removed.

Many of these processes and other, lower-level procedures require either support from or integration with the processes within the security program. Again, Appendix D provides many other examples of processes and procedures that relate to Information Security.

Creating a Successful Security Program

While articulating the security program is difficult enough – people may disagree with some of our terms and definitions – actually developing and maintaining a top-flight program can be daunting. This is especially true if your effort is the organization's first real foray into enterprise-level security. In chapter 1, we outline how to approach building a successful program and share some of our hard-earned tips and tricks on this subject.

A good overall security program is critical to Internet security, and addressing the program along with tactical security initiatives is a best practice. Security dependent on a weak or poorly planned program is like a castle built on sand. Without the strong foundation of a solid program, architecture and infrastructure crumble.

Before diving deeply into this topic, it is helpful to outline, at a high level, the critical issues for creating a successful program. You need to understand the many obstacles that may stand in the way of achieving your objectives.

Elements of the security program will affect everyone in the entire organization. Yet organizations usually have significant inertia. Simple changes to procedures or more significant changes to processes may meet with major resistance. In many cases, there will be deep-seated cultural hurdles to overcome. Even in start-up situations where there may be less organizational inertia, implementing a security program might be held hostage to other pressing priorities. However, we've found you can often overcome these problems if you keep certain security principles in mind.

Key Tenets of a Best Practices Security Program

There are at least four overarching principles to remember when developing the security program. They are as follows:

1. The security program objectives must be tied to business objectives.

2. The security program must have visible executive management support.

3. The program should be measurable and measured over time.

4. The program must follow priorities and manage expectations carefully.

Link Security and Business Objectives

You must make sure your Information Security policy is linked to business objectives. The reason for this is clear. To gain and maintain management support, the security program must be in synch with what business management is trying to accomplish.

Given the wide net that a security program can, and should cast, the costs associated with developing and maintaining it can be sizable. Getting funding and support for the effort is a key initial chore. A security incident that has a large financial consequence or a very public fallout can do wonders for boosting the program budget and fostering a sense of urgency, although we do not recommend taking such a tact as a funding strategy! Rather, you must make a compelling case within your organization for obtaining adequate funding and support. We have found an effective way to accomplish this is to integrate the security program with the business plan.

You should understand the real needs of the business and make sure the security program supports its goals. The security team, in articulating its goals, should employ the same language as the business group. It can tie its goals to strategic business initiatives. This should not be done superficially through the use of a few business buzzwords, but comprehensively, as part of a strategic communications approach.

Linking security to business can be difficult in practice, especially if the organization is undergoing fundamental changes to its mission. It can also be trying in situations where the mission – the actual mission as opposed to what the "mission statement" says – is not clearly communicated nor understood. However, if the security team truly understands the key business initiatives, it can tie them into and obtain funding for some of its own initiatives.

Further, the program should implement both strategic and tactical solutions. As security priorities may not be the same as business priorities, the two need to be reconciled.

Risks Versus Rules

A corollary to this first tenet is that the security program should be risk-based, not rule-based. The idea is not to have a program that throws up a bunch of rules that everyone has to follow. A better long-term approach is to build a risk-based decision framework that lets management reach rational, cost-benefit decisions about security based on the actual security risks to the business. In some cases, management will forego some security measures while accepting the risks. The important thing is to make such a decision overtly, rather than making no decision at all and leaving the acceptance of risk up to chance.

A Case for Funding

A second corollary is that your organization needs a security budget. The best way to obtain an ample security budget is to make the case that the need for security, given the present-day importance of e-Commerce, is vital to the success of the business. (Appendix E identifies trends in security expenditures among organizations.)

Obtain Strong Management Support

The security program must have strong and visible executive management support. This may seem obvious, but we have run into countless situations where there is no clear, forceful backing for a security program. If executive support is absent, obtaining it is one of your first, and possibly most critical, undertakings.

Multiple levels of support are required. An initial key goal, for organizations starting from ground zero, is finding a business sponsor – someone who is a ranking executive, or even better, on the board of directors. Locating an executive willing to play a hands-on role during initial development of the program is also crucial. Indeed, the successful program will have a true "champion," a manager who takes the bull by the horns and sees the program through. This person may or may not be the same as the executive sponsor. And whoever takes on the hands-on role needs to be accessible to all interested parties.

Management support is required in three key areas. First, to communicate the strategy to the rest of the management chain. Second, when developing the program charter, strategy, and initial set of policies, to provide an understanding of the organization's current and future strategy. This will help the security program establish the critical ties to the business mission outlined above. Third, to resolve major differences of opinion within the team during the planning and implementation phases. An executive who is on hand for brief decision sessions can do this.

Employ Measurable and Measured Programs

Given the astonishingly fast ramp-up of network and Internet computing applications, many organizations face serious remedial work to bring their security program up to speed. These conditions demand investment – in many cases a significant expenditure of funds. According to a 1999 META Group study, 79 percent of companies surveyed spend less than $200 per employee on security each year, and 24 percent spend less than $10.

Some of you will be able to open your company's coffers for an initial investment to address the most pressing security problems. However, you will need to find a way to maintain appropriate investments over time. There is no silver bullet solution to that challenge. However, a set of metrics that can substantiate the positive impact of the security program, and prove continuous improvement over time, is an excellent way to begin. In brief, the security program must be measurable and measured over time, otherwise, obtaining funding will be considerably complicated.

Some examples of areas to measure are as follows:

- Reduction in vulnerabilities
- Improved cycle time for new Web application delivery (including security)
- Reduction in incidents or mean time to resolve security incidents (virus, malicious code, denial of service incidents, etc.)
- Percentage of employees who pass a simple security test, or who see a training video

Manage Priorities and Expectations

The stages of the program must be built in priority order. The most important and pressing needs should obviously come first. Further, you need to carefully manage expectations about the program. This tenet is akin to the adage, "Rome wasn't built in a day." Critical to the long-term success of establishing a security program is a phased approach. In most cases, establishing the program and then ratcheting it up to meet the organization's security requirements is a multi-year endeavor. Develop your initial program strategy with this long-range approach in mind. In addition, communicate the long-term strategy to everyone in the program so they can see how the smaller pieces fit into the overall plan.

A pragmatic strategy is to accomplish a mix of strategic and tactical goals through a series of incremental steps. We are not suggesting that you "set the bar low." Instead, we are recommending that you place the bar at an achievable level and then incrementally raise it over time.

Security Program Project Design Considerations

You should take into account practical design considerations when developing the security program. The following list of design considerations is not exhaustive. It addresses some of the most common pitfalls we have encountered.

- When developing the program project strategy and priorities, make sure to garner some "early wins." Nothing generates success like success itself. You can pursue many different strategies in this area, for example, making a marked improvement to a high-visibility vulnerability, helping out with a critical business initiative, or applying a technical solution to a pronounced end user or customer complaint. (A project that reduces sign-on headaches to resolve the ID/password glut).

- Build change management into the program strategy from the start. Change management in this context does not mean the orderly movement of new systems through development, testing and into production. Instead, it refers to the human factor. Changing ingrained behavior, habits, culture, and processes are all part of developing an effective security program. Many people and most organizations are resistant to change. Thus change management must be built into the overall plan.

  One key to effective change management is to involve key groups in the process. We have run into countless situations where the program development team – or even a project team working on a subcomponent of the program – drew up the plan in the back room and then, during the rollout, met with significant opposition. In most cases, the plan was actually fairly sound, but the perception was it was developed in the "ivory tower," and was thus suspect. Often the result was major resistance to the plan and in some cases its outright failure.

  The alternative tactic is to involve people in the design process early on. This fosters a sense of participation and commitment among all parties. However, there is a fine line to walk. Design by committee – especially by a large group – rarely works and often bogs the process down. Developing a project strategy that regularly links key stakeholders to the project can greatly benefit the change management outcome.

- Identify key stakeholders early in the process. This usually requires a strategy that is practical and geared to corporate politics. The process should incorporate a range of individuals from executive management, business, IT, and other groups. You should choose people who are influential in communicating with their peers.

  An alternative, less obvious strategy is to involve a few of the likely "naysayers" or critics of the program. This also involves walking a fine line. Include too many naysayers, and things will go nowhere; select too few, and you'll stand accused of stacking the deck. It is important not only to invite these individuals to the party, but to truly engage them in the design effort so that they share ownership of the work.

  Note many of the specific security processes (for example, incident response), and processes affecting security (such as configuration management) are matrix processes that cut across numerous organizational entities. It is important to integrate those teams into the security program as well.

- Employ a "SWAT team" approach. Many of the business or even IT departments of an organization do not have the expertise or resources to implement the elements of security program recommendation (process changes, new technologies, etc.). We have seen many very well-defined programs languish because there was inadequate expertise or resources to push a new process, procedure, or technology into place. However, a team specially formed to address security can execute the security program while educating the organization's various groups on its work.

Building the Security Program

This section outlines our approach to building a successful program. The overall strategy and some of the specific tactics are designed to avoid or minimize obstacles discussed above.

The program life cycle of the Enterprise-Wide Information Security Program Model represents the top-level phases of implementing and maintaining the security program (refer to Figure 1-3). The diagram illustrates that the security program is a continuous process. Figure 1-7 depicts the steps that organizations typically traverse during their initial program development effort. In addition to the four main phases described in the Security Program Model Life Cycle (assess, design, implement, maintain), you will likely need to add a few additional phases the first time through the life cycle. We discuss some of the project phases below.

Phase 1: Gaining Support

Given the time, people and financial resources necessary to develop a security program, up-front work is necessary to attract an appropriate level of executive support and financial resources. And given the dynamic pace of e-Business and the cost of supporting these efforts, your security team will likely vie for scarce business and executive management time and fight for a slice of the budget.

The objective of this first phase is to get senior management or executive support to analyze the security problem and to make recommendations. It is not necessary or typically even possible to establish funding for the whole effort at this point. It is important to secure funding in Phase 3, assessment.

In addition to obtaining sponsorship for the program, it is important to set expectations on what can be accomplished in this phase and how much it will cost. (See Appendix E for guidance on security costs and budgeting initiatives.)

There is no single recipe for gaining executive support for security program initiatives. Similar strategies are likely to have different results from organization to organization. However, some of the tactics that have worked well with a number of our clients are as follows:

1. **Top-Down Tactics** – These tactics require some solid business knowledge and, usually, support and involvement from your department's senior management. It is aimed at one or more of the organization's senior executives, for example, the president or executive vice president.

   1A. *Scared Straight by "Ethical Hacking"* – Fear tends to be a good motivator. "Smoking gun" evidence of how vulnerable the organization is to external attack can be a definite attention grabber. Further, senior managers have a corporate responsibility to act on this type of information when it is brought to their attention.

   There are multiple ways and price tags to execute this tactic. (The idea at this point is not to find every vulnerability, but to focus attention on the security issue itself). Many consulting agencies can do a limited scope vulnerability assessment on, for example, your network perimeter. The cost is very reasonable, ranging from $10,000 - $40,000, depending on organizational size, complexity, depth of analysis, etc. A key consideration is to ensure that whoever does the work can take a very technical assessment and translate it into terms that the business management can

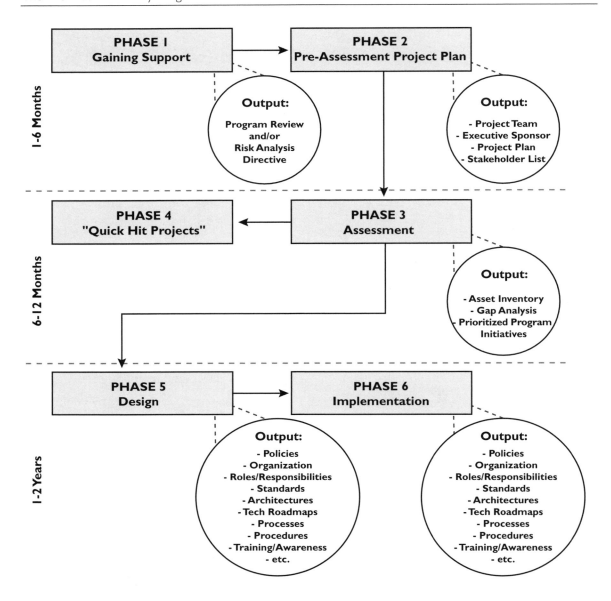

Figure 1-7: Phases of a First-Time Security Program

understand. In a similar vein, the assessment must link the security issues back to the business. It should demonstrate the impact that vulnerabilities might have on the organization's information assets, business operations, etc.

An alternative is a very inexpensive, external vulnerability scan ranging from $1000 - $5,000. This is affectionately know in security consulting circles as "a scan with a cover letter." Typically, it consists of a report that is merely the output of a commercial vulnerability scanning tool, plus a brief cover letter. One downside to this method is the lack of a business tie-in. A techie, jargon-filled report can actually have a negative result, namely, a loss of credibility with senior management. Thus, you need to spend some time tuning the report to link it to business issues. Finally, as a "cheap and dirty" method, there are freeware tools that can be used to perform an initial vulnerability scanning. This method has the same risk as the prior option, so making sure the results get translated into business terms is key. A few examples of this tool include:

- NMAP (www.insecure.org) – Reconnaissance tool typically used for mapping networks, discovering what network services are running (and are potentially exposed), and finding what operating systems are available.

- Nessus (www.nessus.org) – UNIX-based vulnerability scanning tool that is kept up-to-date by the open source security community (both white hat and black hat elements).

- LOphtCrack (www.atstake.com) – LC3, the latest version of LOphtCrack, for sniffing, stealing, and cracking NT passwords using brute force methods (which try every password combination), or dictionary methods (which crack common passwords by matching possibly valid entries to an online dictionary).

- Packetstorm (packetstorm.securify.com) – Web site containing information on many freeware tools.

1B. *Safety in Small Numbers* – We have been particularly successful in working with executive teams in small group settings. We hold one- to three-hour seminars on new Information Security risks and their business consequences.

Executive awareness sessions work well under these conditions: 1) they are limited to a small group of executives (2 to 15 in number), who do not have any security-related political agendas; 2) the presenter/moderator is a businessman, not a "techno weenie"; and 3) the presentation and discussion start and end with business-related concerns.

To great effect, we have tied in cracker demos to illustrate the actual dangers and to entertain the audience members – they tend not to forget what they see! The cracker demo – a combination of breach scenarios and screen shots of popular cracker Web haunts – usually connects with a non-technical audience only if it uses down-to-earth, physical security analogies as opposed to emphasizing technical details.

1C. *Scared Straight by a Guilty Conscience* – This method stokes executive interest by referring to new or outstanding audit points (for example, an SAS-70 audit), or new or existing regulations or legislation (such as the new HIPPA federal health care requirements). This technique can be used in conjunction with other tactics.

1D. *Business Logic Argument* – It is particularly difficult to make the case that Information Security can actually provide a company with competitive advantages. The very few rare exceptions are situations where confidentiality, integrity, etc. are the top two or three buying considerations for the majority of the organization's customers. However, Information Security, or rather the lack thereof, can definitely place an organization at a competitive disadvantage. A financial organization with a solid security program enjoys significant time-to-market advantages if it can roll out new e-Business applications faster than its competitors. A firm with less robust security faces the choice of waiting for security to come up to speed or implementing an insecure system with significant risks.

In light of increasing customer privacy concerns, this factor may grow in importance, especially for business Web sites, given the spurt of recent, headline-grabbing Denial of Service (DoS) attacks. A Web-based enterprise is like a cyber cash register – if it stops ringing due to a DoS outage, competitors will be eager to pick up the slack.

1E. *The Herd Logic Argument* – Best practice comparisons with competitors are often a good way to elicit interest. This relatively cheap method requires some Web surfing time – to gather press clippings about what competitors are doing or what security breaches have afflicted them. Other useful sources of information are conferences and other industry gatherings where listening to presentations or talking to attendees can yield insights about the security efforts of competitors.

2. **Bottoms-Up Efforts** – IT management should take a careful approach to eliciting support for security from management. Going directly to senior business management can be a "career-limiting" move. A middle way is better: gaining support through a consensus of middle-level managers, followed by concerted "upselling" up the chain of management. The eventual aim is to garner the support of high management for top-down initiatives. In some organizations, the IT organization is able to obtain the necessary funding without top-down tactics, but in many cases, the budget required to fund program-level initiatives is substantial enough to warrant the top-down approach.

3. **Riding the Train** – Hitching the Information Security program to a high-profile project train is a good, backhanded method of funding all or part of the security program initiative. The idea is to find a high-profile business/technology initiative and siphon off some funds from it. Some projects are big enough (for example, the SAP projects of the mid- to late-90s, or a large new e-business initiative) that even allotting a rather large chunk for security program development is hardly noticeable.

Security is usually a concern for e-business applications. Thus, creatively procuring some extra funding for program-level initiatives may not be too difficult. This can be a risky move, however, as senior management does not always look favorably at such budgetary stratagems.

Phase 2: Pre-assessment Project Planning

Like all large projects, developing a security program requires an overall plan. Thus, a critical first step is to "plan the plan." The assumption is that you have already garnered some level of management support and funding for the effort.

The main goal of this phase is to develop a project and project team that can succeed. Planning for success may seem a simplistic way of portraying the Phase 2 goal, but many of the failures that we see result from creating a project plan that fails to factor in the issues and design criteria discussed in the previous sections.

The outputs of this phase are as follows:

- Project team and team role definitions
- Project sponsor and role definition
- Key stakeholder list
- Detailed project plan for the assessment phase

Identifying the appropriate project team is a critical step and a common pitfall. Choosing a team that can execute the roles and accomplish the project is obviously important. However, as discussed earlier, selecting individuals who can sell the recommendations, and making choices to mitigate or even to recruit potential naysayers, are key considerations.

Having a multi-disciplinary team is a must, and some of the skill requirements likely require members from outside of the existing security team, the IT group, and possibly even the organization itself. This is not a thinly veiled way of selling you on external consultants (we'll get to that later). Rather, it is a simple recognition that a rock-solid project team is crucial. Solid project management skills and an aptitude for conducting interviews and facilitated sessions are possibly the most difficult roles to fill. Since the assessment phase includes interviews with business and IT employees from all levels in the organization, finding someone who can act as a strong leader for these sessions is critical. After all, these early interview sessions establish a positive or negative image of the overall project.

Deciding which stakeholders to interview is also key. It is important to get feedback during the assessment phase from various levels of the organization. We talk more about choosing stakeholders during our discussion on policy development in chapter two.

Phase 3: Assessment

The assessment phase is designed to review – at a high-level – the current state of key Information Security program issues. An important goal is to compare the current state to the desired future state, and develop a prioritized set of initiatives to bridge the gap between the two.

This phase typically has three steps:

1. Data collection (current state and desired future state)
2. Program gap analysis
3. Reporting

The goals of the assessment phase include:

- Understand current enterprise security risks as they relate to current and future business goals.

- Understand especially serious vulnerabilities to critical systems.

- Understand systemic issues (process, procedural, organizational, governance, etc.) that tend to be the root cause of the vulnerabilities.

- Understand the business strategy, how it relates to future plans, and how security can support the strategy.

- Understand program implementation challenges.

- Understand political and other obstacles that can impact rollout.

- Begin the change management process.

- Understand the next-year priorities (from an information risk management perspective). There are likely both strategic and tactical issues to address.

- Gain consensus on findings, recommendations, and an action plan.

- Gain approval and a budget for moving forward with quick hitters and more strategic plans.

Data Collection

There are three major areas of data that need to be collected to perform the GAP analysis.

The first is information about the current and future direction of the business. This is typically done through a review of the documentation for current business planning/strategy, and through interviews with key senior managers. The best practice is to engage in both one-on-one sessions and in facilitated sessions with senior business managers from corporate, from business divisions or departments, and from field management. (If you actually get a truly consistent story about exactly where the business is going, please call the Harvard Business Review and give them the scoop.) Find out what these key stakeholders view as their critical assets, their level of risk tolerance, and the importance of Information Security to their business goals.

The second area of data collection is the current state of security at the organization. This includes both the current risk profile, as well as a review of the major security program elements (policies, procedures, standards, processes, organization/governance, technology). In reviewing the security program elements, the goal is to understand where they stand relative to good practice, or best practice. That is, if these are practiced at all!

For the risk review portion of the data collection exercise, we recommend a statistically relevant vulnerability and threat analysis. We believe, often in stark contrast to others in the industry, that it is best to do some sort of Information Security risk review on just a subset of the organization. Our justification is simplistic: spend more money on fixing problems than assessing them.

Exhaustive enterprise-wide assessments can be very expensive; many of these reports collect dust as the team waits for new funding because the assessment ate the budget. Assessing headquarters, other very large sites, and a select sampling of smaller, more remote sites should suffice. (We realize of course that the "size" of a facility is relative, depending on the organization.) Unless you already have a very sophisticated security program – in which case you should be at the beach instead of reading this report – or the disposable assets of Bill Gates, an exhaustive review of every part of the organization is not required. You can obtain good results from a small sampling of systems rather than the whole portfolio. Still, examining the most critical systems is a must. These are usually easy to identify through the disaster recovery plan or the old Y2K contingency plan. And checking a few systems of lesser importance gives you a well-rounded view.

The third area of data collection is discussed in the following section.

Security Program Gap Analysis

"Gap" analysis defines the difference or gap between the current state and the desired future state of security. In this analysis the focus is on the desired future state, or best practice – which is the third area of data collection. The truly hard part about the gap analysis is actually figuring out what industry best practice is. As the preface of this report implied, there is no magic database in the sky for good or best practice. This endeavor is further complicated by the industry hype that vendor marketing organizations push regarding various new technologies. If you were to listen only to vendors, you'd believe everyone everywhere is using PKI, or will be tomorrow, or every organization is monitoring all their systems for intruders – to use a few technology-centric examples.

Inaccurate information on where the industry is relative to security technology adoption is pervasive, but the thornier issue is that information on some of the program elements can be very hard to dig up. For a group within an organization, it takes a concerted effort to characterize what best or even good practice is. There are many sources of information, but culling through them takes time, and even then the picture will be incomplete.

Still, some good sources exist. They include the following:

1. **Industry analyst firms who can strip out some of the vendor hype.** (Examples are META Group, Gartner Group, Forrester Research) Many of their reports are forward-looking, but their analysts are often knowledgeable of current technology, too. The better ones also understand the current state of the other program elements.

2. **Industry conferences and other people-networking events.** Chatting with attendees and lecturers can elicit solid, realistic information on the industry.

3. **The network and security media.** There are some very good publications that provide a level-headed picture of industry best practice, but beware of some of the sensational stories that the IT press covers. The tendency is to give lots of play to new and advanced items, or bleeding-edge organizations that are more "new practice," rather than best practice.

4. **Outside consultants.** So here it comes, the unadulterated plug. In many cases, it is valuable to use an outside consulting firm for information about best practices – for example, say some observers, a company like METASeS. Through numerous project engagements, firms like ours pick up data points on what is good and best practice. Outside consulting firms are not a panacea, however. *Caveat emptor* (buyer beware). Selecting a vendor – and the specific team to do the work – requires doing your homework and exercising sound judgment.

Reporting

In performing our Information Security assessments, we often find the various organizations have similar issues and concerns to be addressed. This is especially true for firms that are just beginning to reexamine security due to the rising Internet threat.

Some of the most common security program issues that a gap analysis typically uncovers are as follows:

- Unclear governance for Information Security. There is often lax or fuzzy responsibility and accountability for all aspects of Information Security within the organization.

- Very weak, or non-existent, security awareness training

- Non-existent, ill-defined, or poorly communicated Information Security policy, standards, and procedures and processes

Note that Appendix A provides a sample gap analysis report from a typical Information Security program assessment.

Priorities

One of the most important aspects of the report is to develop a solid road map for the initiatives required to improve the security program. Possibly the single most important aspect of this endeavor is how well the initiatives are prioritized. Pursuing a series of smaller-scale projects, rather than grand, all-encompassing efforts, is also critical. Getting a security program up to scratch often takes a year or more – notwithstanding incremental improvements – so doing the correct things first is very important.

These "correct" things have two aspects. During the facilitated sessions and one-on-one meetings with management, you will undoubtedly pick up on some issues that the attendees believe are pressing. This concern may very well stem from a near-term business project that relies on some aspect of security, or from a specific, current problem – for example, "too darn many passwords to remember."

Phase 4: Quick Hit Projects

As shown in phase 4 in Figure 1-7, it is important to find some "quick hitter" projects to build momentum and credibility for future, more important, longer-running security initiatives. Finding a few small projects that can have some incrementally positive impact is an important success factor. To use password security as an example, we would not recommend trying something like an enterprise-wide single sign-on initiative. A more prudent alternative would be to leverage a network conversion project or a directory project to reduce the password load in some specific systems. Another example would be to improve the risk posture of a critical Web application. Keep two things in mind about quick hitters. Watch carefully for these kind of quick-fix opportunities during the data-gathering portion of the phase, and appropriately advertise the quick hitters upon their successful completion.

The risk management formula, *Risk = Threat x Vulnerability x Asset Value*, can be a good guide for establishing priorities. You can generate a road map by moving through the equation from right to left, examining the most important things first. That is, focus first on protecting the assets with the highest value. Another key priority at this juncture is identifying critical vulnerabilities or major classes of vulnerabilities affecting the critical assets.

In addition, as with assets, some vulnerabilities are more important than others. Vulnerabilities on a network perimeter, which can enable external attacks, or on a subnetwork housing a critical system, are relatively more important. Further, some vulnerabilities are easier to exploit than others – a physical analogy would be an unlocked front door, which is more exposed than a bolted, out-of-view cellar door. Moving further left in the equation, you can see that some vulnerabilities and even some assets are not as important because there is no threat (people, organization, etc.) that is likely to exploit them. In practice, it is not always easy to do this kind of rank ordering of priorities. Nonetheless, the risk formula can be a very good mechanism to help focus your attention on the prioritization task.

Phases 5 and 6: Implementation and Design

Some of the typical next-year priorities undertaken in phases 5 and 6 are:

- Update policy, standards, procedures – Review and refine policies and technical security standards/procedures, especially those for hardening high-risk technologies (systems on the perimeter network or those supporting very critical systems). This typically includes addressing new Internet-related issues, for example malicious code, and acceptable use of new Internet resources (browsing, e-mail, remote access, etc.)

- Develop and deploy an Information Security awareness program – Because user-related vulnerabilities are typically a critical issue, especially in an Internet era of malicious attacks (the "I Love You" bug, the Melissa derivatives, Back Orifice, rogue applets, etc.), getting the word out is a priority.

- Develop at least a preliminary security incident response capability – With the likelihood of security exploits rising, establishing a team that can respond to and minimize damage is often a necessity.

- Appoint a corporate-level Chief Security Officer (CSO) responsible for enterprise-wide Information Security – This step is becoming popular with many organizations.

Conclusion

Assessing the multidimensional Information Security area can be daunting. It would be relatively easy to address any one of the program elements, but the possible end result would be to ignore another aspect of the problem or miss a critical concern. Thus, even if an organization does a good job at fixing identified problem areas, it remains at an unacceptable level of risk.

It could also be easy to think of Phases 1-3 as separate and distinct from Phases 4-6, where solutions to problems are devised and implemented. However, since much of the success of a security program hinges on modifying behavior, it is absolutely critical to use Phases 1-3 not only to identify issues, but to begin the change management process – changing behavior through awareness, education, and involvement.

A vital concern is which projects receive attention after assessment. You want to remove some current problem areas through a few quick hitters, and then focus attention on priority projects. This method will have the most demonstrable effect on an organization's Information Security risk profile. To reemphasize, quick hitters and priority projects are critical success factors.

Finally, the ultimate success or failure of the effort will likely hinge on garnering enough executive support and on staffing the project with a select and capable team.

Developing an Information Security Policy 2

The practice of Information Security has become the business of managing risk. The more important something is, the more it must be protected, and that is certainly the case with information in the modern Internet marketplace. Security is, in the end, another form of business risk, and it must be managed in the same way that other business risks are analyzed and weighed.

Information Security policies provide the broad rules for ensuring the protection of information assets and for implementing a security program. Policies impart the organization's high-level Information Security philosophy. Generally brief in length, policies are independent of particular technologies and the details of specific solutions. They should remain relevant and applicable for a substantial period of time until the organization's security objectives or concerns change.

A policy may identify the following:

- Its general features and objectives
- Its scope (the areas requiring policy coverage)
- The parties responsible for performing the Information Security functions in the policy coverage area
- Consequences of violating the policy
- Provisions for handling exceptions to the policy

Information Security policy establishes the charter for the security program and the rules that govern security within the organization. It takes on a very important role in the security program in general and network and Internet security in particular. It provides a key link back to the organization's goals. Information security policy is the foundation of any security infrastructure. It can be tricky to develop and keep up to date. For all these reasons, this chapter presents a full discussion of policy.

Policies operate hand-in-hand with standards and procedures. Standards define the acceptable level of security for a specific, associated policy area. An example of a standard is a requirement that each user have a unique user ID and password. Standards provide measurable criteria for satisfying high-level objectives defined in the policy. Each policy may have one or more associated standards. Procedures give specific, step-by-step advice on how to implement the standards.

The right Information Security policy provides your organization with a concise, high-level strategy to shape your tactical security solutions. It will clearly define the value of your information assets, represent organization-wide priorities, and state definitively the underlying assumptions that drive security activities. By going through the process of developing a relevant, usable policy, you can make the hard decisions on the security program up front, making implementation of the rest of the program that much easier. In contrast, building security "solutions" that are not based on sound, well-thought-out policy, but on quick technological "fixes," may just result in the purchase of a lot of expensive hardware.

You may be wondering why we're spending two chapters explaining the importance of security programs and policies before getting into the "nitty gritty" of security architecture and infrastructure. The answer: Policy, although often overlooked, is absolutely critical. Your organization can have the best security architecture and infrastructure, but still have lousy security if your policy is poorly drawn up and put into practice. Having bad policy or no policy, while buying a raft of the latest security infrastructure such as firewalls and Web servers, is like having cops, courts, and prisons, but no laws.

So a key question remains: Is your policy adequate to deal with today's rapidly changing IT environment? Many companies initiating electronic business efforts are finding their existing policies are either woefully outdated, or have been developed in bits and pieces over time – they don't have a coherent security strategy that accurately reflects their current needs. That is, assuming that they have a policy at all! A 1999 *Information Week* Research Global Information Security Survey of 2,700 security professionals world-wide found that 19 percent of respondents had no security policy and 59 percent did not believe that their policies strongly matched their business objectives. Fewer than one third described their policies as highly effective (Figure 2-1).

Developing a good Information Security policy means a commitment of time and effort, but it pays off in several important ways. The old adage, "If you fail to plan, then you are planning to fail" certainly applies here. When you don't have or don't follow a policy, employee oversight can leave information systems and other resources unprotected, or you can spend money to protect the wrong resources. By following a formal policy, however, you are far more likely to provide security appropriate to the value of the assets being protected.

A formal security policy clarifies higher-level organizational objectives. It thus serves as a guideline for employees' routine, day-to-day, security-related activities. System administrators can make decisions based on the information in the policy and can rely on the policy document to support their decisions. Time is saved and work is better focused. For example, clearly defined responsibilities can help system administrators know whether a requested software application is allowed, or precisely who must be contacted to obtain approval.

The Information Security policy also plays a critical role in liability abatement. The very fact your organization has gone through the entire process of creating a security policy demonstrates a significant level of due diligence in the protection of its information assets and the assets of others such as customers, for which it may have a stewardship role. Fully disseminating the security policy document within the organization can further limit liability.

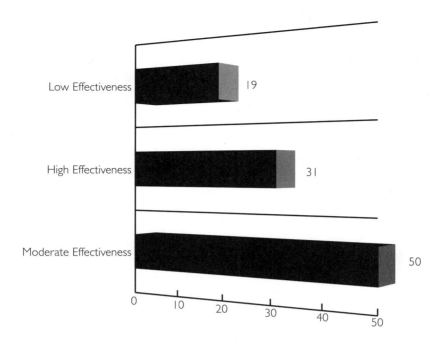

Figure 2-1: Reported Effectiveness of Current Information Security Policy

The Impact of the Internet

In recent years, businesses have had to face the challenge of a major computing paradigm shift – from proprietary networks and system architectures to "open systems" with distributed, heterogeneous servers and clients. Formerly, data was stored and managed on mainframes and centralized clusters of smaller systems. Strong host-based controls provided significant assurance that information resources were protected from unauthorized access, disclosure, or modification. Users and managers took it for granted that Information Security was adequately addressed. However, the move to internal and Internet-based TCP/IP networks, as well as to distributed computing based on desktop PCs or remotely-connected laptops, has reduced the effectiveness of traditional controls. The factors for this include the following:

- The communication medium that connects users to data is very likely part of a publicly accessible information access system like the Internet.

- Proximity no longer determines access – legitimate users can be anywhere.

- Data is not necessarily located in a single location or a centrally controlled system: data may be in many locations and have multiple copies.

The rapid growth of the Internet has coincided with the trend toward the "virtual corporation," where the lines between businesses and their customers, suppliers, partners and agents are increasingly blurred. The currency of the new digital economy is information and intellectual capital, neither of which has value unless it is shared. Companies are not only making information available outside their own networks, they are allowing outsiders in to view or update information. The Internet is not the corporate data center yet, but things are certainly moving in that direction. Business-critical applications can be hosted by third-party providers, remote file storage can be rented, and even e-mail can be outsourced. Commerce is rapidly becoming a network of digital transactions that must be defined and controlled through the use of contracts, agreements, and policy. New tools and practices – addressed in chapter 3 – are necessary to support the strategic business and policy objectives.

Consequently, networks and the business relationships they support must be dynamic and flexible. The Internet has lowered the barriers to entry for many players, both geographically and in time to market. All markets are now international and, indeed, parts of the global economy now exist solely in cyberspace. From a technical perspective, this situation means the model of the "secure perimeter" – where, in effect, a "castle wall" surrounds a network and a firewall guards the sole access point – is essentially dead. It has been replaced by a distributed environment where data is far more open to access by both legitimate and illegitimate users (see Figure 2-2).

The Internet environment is riskier than previous business environments because there is much more to lose. There is more to gain, too, but participating in the online marketplace requires new security approaches for user access controls and data protection. The enormous increase in data sharing means a concurrent need for intelligent regulation of information. In such a milieu, the need for well-defined, carefully considered policy is greater than ever, and in fact may be a prerequisite for doing business.

The rest of this section outlines the characteristics of and a process for defining sound policy, and for successfully promulgating it throughout your organization. Policy needs may vary considerably from one organization to the next, but the basic process will be the same.

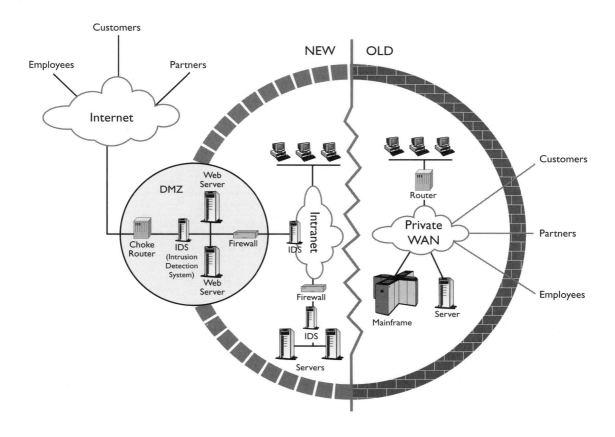

Figure 2-2: Old & New Views of Security Permeability

Characteristics of Good Information Security Policy

We have found through long experience with clients a useful, workable Information Security policy has a number of the following characteristics:

- The policy should clearly delineate responsibility, accountability, and lines of authority across the organization. These provide a solid definition of what is expected of people inside and outside of the organization, and outline exactly how to accomplish these expectations. These are reflected in employment contracts, job specifications, job output models, performance reviews, disciplinary codes, etc.

- One of the most important characteristics is the scope of the policy. As early as possible in the process, you should define what corporate resources it affects, and to whom the policy applies – all employees, full-time employees only, contractors, consultants, or customers. Based on your organization's hierarchy and location, you may need to develop different policies for different groups or locales.

- The policy should be restricted in its reach and clear in its organization. It should be limited to stating the organization's security objectives, priorities, and high-level strategies, thus serving as a framework for the various business areas. It should be concise and written in clear, unambiguous language that speaks directly to a broad audience. It should be carefully structured to allow easy reference to particular sections. Remember: not everyone is a lawyer, nor has a degree in computer science.

- The policy should focus exclusively on broad principles. It is intended as a living reference document, for use over a long period. Every contingency or every implementation detail cannot be foreseen. Details on how to apply the policy to areas that are more often updated, such as individual business practices or computing resources, should be addressed in separate acceptable use documents or procedure manuals.

- The policy document must be carefully worded. It is very important to ensure all terms are accurately and precisely defined and used exactly as intended. Each concept should be carefully but broadly defined, not in relation to a particular technology.

- As a living document, the policy should be reviewed at regular intervals, or as events, such as a merger or an acquisition, require. It should be flexible enough to deal with new and rapidly changing technology landscapes without having to be constantly rewritten. It should be modular enough to modify fairly easily without sparking a cascade of required changes.

- The various constituents governed by the policy should see only the material they need to see rather than being required to read and understand all of the policy information. This will improve compliance with the policy. While "ignorance of the law" should not excuse its violation, practicality suggests that a more minimalist approach to policy is preferred. With this approach, personnel will actually understand what matters most in the performance of their jobs.

- To give the policy document clout, both senior management and users must accept it as the official reference document on policy. The document should be introduced with a statement from a senior individual who confirms top management's commitment to the policy principles.

- The policy should firmly integrate Information Security policy within the overall business and technical strategies, and within risk management practices.

- The business should drive the policy and policy enforcement, not the other way around.

- The policy must be consistent with existing corporate directives and guidelines, and with applicable government legislation and regulations.

- The policy must be technically and organizationally feasible. It must take a realistic approach to what can be accomplished with current technology, or to what is practical for procedural enforcement, within the constraints of the organization's culture and mission. A security policy will likely have little to do with technology or with what it alone can accomplish.

- The policy should establish requirements for a review process for new technologies and activities. This should ensure the infrastructures necessary to identify, monitor, and control Information Security risks prior to their introduction.

- Each policy should clearly describe how exceptions to the policy are considered and adjudicated.

- The initial policy document, and subsequent updates, should have a version number and a date. We recommend you maintain all policy documents in a centrally managed change control system that keeps a log of modifications.

METASeS Information Security Policy Framework

We've found that there is a lot more to Information Security policy than just policy itself. There's a host of related topics like technical standards and procedures.

During the past year, our Research & Development team has been working to define a new piece of important intellectual property. We call it the METASeS Information Security Policy Framework™.

Information Security Policy Framework Goals

Our goal in creating an Information Security Policy Framework was to provide a "best practice" model that you could use to perform the following:

- Assess your current Information Security polices, and perform a gap analysis against our "best practice" reference model to highlight necessary improvements.

- Provide a baseline reference model that you could customize to address your organization's unique needs – based on its business requirements, culture, industry regulations, etc.

Our initial aim was simply to develop a best practice security policy reference model. However, as we progressed in our effort, we broadened the scope to a policy framework. This covers not only policy itself, but also accounts for policy-related components and related items including technical standards, processes, and procedures. Thus, we ended up developing an Information Security Policy Framework ttraceable back to key Information Security tenets and an organization's business or mission goals. (More on this last point later.)

How We Arrived at Our Framework

Figure 2-3 illustrates the process we took to develop the METASeS Information Security Policy Framework.

Our R&D team started by defining security objectives. Then we undertook an exhaustive review of literature in the policy area. We collectively reviewed everything we could find on the topic, including research papers from government and commercial sources, commentary published on the Web, and various books (see Appendix C). We were fortunate to have had many very talented pioneers who preceded us in this well-documented area. They include the likes of Thomas R. Peltier, Charles Cresson Woods, and Donn Parker.

We also spent countless hours "in the cave." In our precious spare moments, we consultants engage in research and writing work that is not specifically part of customer service. These review, development, and quality assurance sessions yielded many of the ideas for the Framework.

Because there were volumes written on the subject, and since our team has collectively completed innumerable policy assessment and development projects with customers, an obvious question was: Why would we need to develop our own framework? Instead, why not simply recycle some of the existing work? The truth of the matter is that we started out on that path, and in fact ended up liberally reusing much of the prior work, including that of the pioneers mentioned above. However, as we got together to discuss the topic in detail, it became clear that all of the team members, as

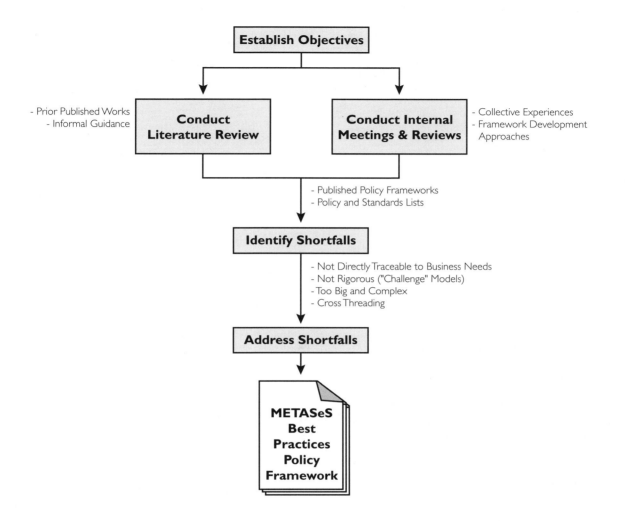

Figure 2-3: Process for Developing the METASeS Best Practices Policy Framework

they worked with clients over the past decade, had consistently run into novel issues with existing frameworks.

These issues included:

1. Not really knowing whether our work was done – In past projects we continually ran into this "done or not" problem. We were never positive that we had covered all the bases, especially at the top level. In fact, you are never really done with policy since it requires ongoing maintenance, but knowing when and whether you had initially covered all of the necessary issues was a thorny problem. In each of the policy reference models, we looked at, and even in our own previous models, we were not able to establish a clear finish line.

That is not to say that we and others before us didn't provide customers with a quality work product. Our work and many of the models we reviewed passed rigorous quality review cycles from many of the top minds in the industry. However, with all the other previous models, the "proof" always took the form of a challenge model. That is, the completeness of the work was not subject to a formal proof. Rather, its comprehensiveness was typically tested by a challenge such as, "We'll see if you can find any holes in what we came up with." This challenge model gnawed at us because we were unable to demonstrate beyond a doubt the completeness of our work – even if we could hold off any accusations of its inadequacy.

2. Cross-threaded definitions – With both our prior work and that of others, we continuously ran into problems with policy component definitions. Especially in practice, the definitions for policy and their cousins – standards, procedure, process, guidelines, etc. – tended to have many shades of interpretation. Various pieces of the model were sometimes used synonymously. Other times, they were used to convey different things, but were often not defined well enough to show how each piece differed, where it fit in the picture, and why it was needed. (The Preface discusses the difficulty of coming up with consistent definitions.)

Given our years of experience in the field, we had no illusions about defining a new *de facto*, industry-wide definition set for policy frameworks. As battle-hardened consultants, we were strongly biased toward actual practice rather than pointy-headed academic musings. However, in this case we needed to provide clear baseline definitions so we could effectively perform assessments and provide substantive structural recommendations. During our policy assessment projects, we have always been able to make substantial recommendations on content – for writing style, completeness of an individual policy, ability to audit, etc. However, we often had issues with the overall organization of the client's policy material. Such items were typically very easy to point out, but difficult to articulate in a clear set of remedial recommendations.

3. Traceability – As all of the pioneers in this field have pointed out, the policy used to frame Information Security discussion hinges on the organization's business or mission rather than the other way around. To that end, we struggled with just how to provide a direct line of logic between top-level policy, the other framework components, and the business and mission goals they support. Our challenge was to pick a relevant starting point for policy that would enable direct traceability through each component of the framework.

Policy Framework Concepts

As the METASeS Information Security Policy Framework took shape, we developed some new concepts to meet the aforementioned security goals and characteristics. (See the section Characteristics of Good Information Security Policy above).

The concepts include the following:

- Tying policy directly to a risk management formula that traces directly back to specific business requirements.

- A hierarchy of policy elements to directly link the various policies with the risk formula (refer to Figure I-5), and in turn, with other framework elements – standards, procedures, and guidelines. Thus, the items at lower levels in the framework are associated with the risk equation and traceable back to business objectives.

- The notion of policy interpretations as a vehicle for addressing various requirements, including the following:

- How to adapt to new technology without having to make wholesale changes or additions to existing policy. For example, a policy interpretation for the Internet, an intranet, extranet, or an e-mail system, etc., would enable organizations to explain what needs to be done – from a policy, standards, procedures perspective – to address the risks such new technologies pose to the organization.

- How to organize the Information Security policy, including its related components, for various constituencies within and outside the organization, rather than writing totally new unrelated documents for each of them.

- How to maintain a minimum set of policies, thus simplifying their understanding by all personnel, while still making specific constituencies aware of policy elements that apply to them or to a certain technology arena.

- The notion of a guideline as a standard in waiting, rather than another level in the policy framework hierarchy – we found the concept of a guideline sprinkled throughout many earlier policy works. However, they tended to have only "referential definitions." Many organizations require this loose kind of definition to be able to deal with new and not very well defined, technologies. For example, in the early days of e-mail, an organization could have defined a guideline on it prior to developing a complete and thorough set of standards and procedures to reduce the risk of the technology. A guideline and a standard are analogous to a proposed piece of legislation and an actual law.

While a perfect policy framework cannot reduce risk by itself (just as perfect security technology cannot), a clearly defined and substantiated policy framework strengthens Information Security while minimizing its cost.

METASeS Information Security Policy Framework Best Practices

As shown in Figure 2-4, the METASeS Policy Framework includes a capstone Information Security Program Charter, plus seven named policy areas.

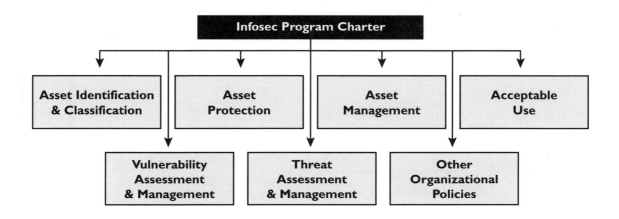

Figure 2-4: METASeS Best Practices Policy Framework

The policy areas are:

1. Asset Identification and Classification
2. Asset Protection
3. Asset Management
4. Acceptable Use
5. Vulnerability Assessment and Management
6. Threat Assessment and Management
7. Other Organizational Policies

The Information Security Charter and the first six policy areas are discussed in separate sections below.

The seventh policy category is reserved for Other Organization Policies (that is, those normally defined, developed, and managed outside of the Information Security organization, but which have a direct bearing on Information Security). Code of Ethics and Incident Recovery are examples of Other Organizational Policies.

Figure 2-5 shows how the risk management variables trace down to the foundational "policy areas" shown under Assets, Vulnerabilities, and Threats.

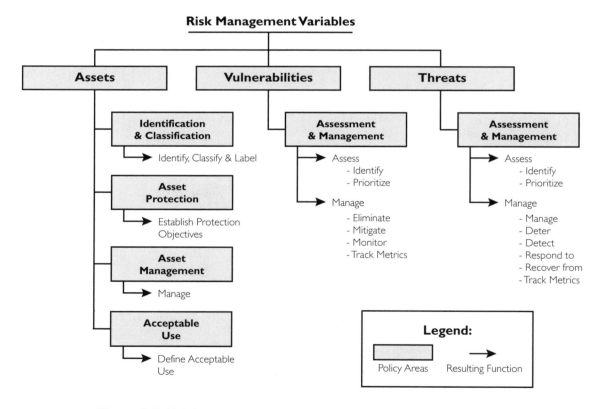

Figure 2-5: Link Between Risk Management Objectives & Resulting Functions

The foundational policies – for assets, threats, and vulnerabilities – are broken out in the sections that follow.

Assets

To address the asset aspect of risk, your organization must do the following:

- Identify and classify its assets.

- Establish protection objectives for the assets.

- Manage the assets.

- Define acceptable use of the assets.

Vulnerabilities

To address the vulnerability aspect of risk, your organization must assess, identify, prioritize, and manage vulnerabilities. The management activities must support organizational objectives for mitigating the vulnerabilities as well as developing and using metrics to gauge improvements or setbacks.

Threats

To address the threat aspect of risk, the organization must assess, identify, monitor, and prioritize threats. The monitoring activities must support organizational objectives for deterring, responding to, and recovering from threat activity. The monitoring activities also must support, as with the vulnerabilities aspect of risk, the development and use of metrics to gauge improvements or shortfalls.

The following sections summarize the topical coverage provided by the Information Security Charter, and each of the six foundational Information Security policies (Figures 2-4 and 2-5).

Information Security Charter

The Information Security Charter is the capstone of the policy framework. It empowers the security program to manage Information Security-related business risks. The charter is basically the mission statement for the Information Security program, and establishes how to support critical business objectives. The charter also outlines key program management issues, including the following:

- **Executive ownership** – This identifies the high-level executive with responsibility for Information Security.

- **Management responsibility** – This pertains to who is responsible for various aspects of the Information Security program, and for ongoing updates to the policy framework.

- **Accountability for integrity and security of assets** – This pertains to the person responsible for integrity of the assets. He can, and often should, be different from the persons responsible for executive ownership and management responsibility.

- **Scope of coverage** – A high-level description of which assets, people, and organizations are governed by the policy framework.

- **Policy enforcement** – This includes consequences for non-compliance, and methods for exception handling.

- **Communication of the security program and policy framework** – This entails how and to whom policy is transmitted within the organization.

Asset Identification and Classification

The asset identification and classification policy allows an organization to better leverage future investments in security and risk management efforts by focusing on critical information assets and by providing a level of security appropriate to the value of the assets. In short, you are far more likely to get the best return on investment for your security expenditures when you have consciously determined what assets require protection, and to what degree.

Asset identification may seem like a trivial exercise. This is certainly not the case! While the specific definition of assets will vary from organization to organization, assets generally may include:

- Raw Data
- Information (Processed Data)
- Systems
- Networks
- Processes
- People
- Other Business Enablers (e.g., reputation, trust, and other "social" assets)

The asset identification and classification policy provides the governance necessary to define and identify organizational assets. After your organization identifies its assets (independent of how this was done), it must prioritize their importance. The prioritization is essential to the process of defining risk management priorities. In practice, the prioritization activities should result in assets being placed into one of a number, say three to five, classifications of importance. These provide a basis for other Information Security standards. (For example, incident response standards may reference these asset classifications and define specific responses for each.)

Asset Protection

The asset protection policy provides the governance necessary to establish specific standards on the appropriate degree of confidentiality, integrity, and availability for your organization's assets. Note that the asset protection policy in the Best Policy Framework is a "superset" of narrow policies, such as authorization and authentication. METASeS believes policies should provide strategic governance and considers authorization and similar topics as more detailed, "how to" subjects for achieving the central goals of confidentiality, integrity, and availability.

Asset Management

The asset management policy provides the governance necessary to define asset stewardship, as well as change control and configuration management objectives throughout the asset life cycle. Asset stewardship simply means that each asset should have a clearly defined steward. A steward is the person who, while not necessarily the owner of data, has the ultimate responsibility for its proper handling and safekeeping. In the absence of regulatory requirements (or authorized assignment of responsibility to another person or organization), the steward is responsible for defining and coordinating protection objectives.

In practice, assets may be "nested" within the IT environment. For example, an online banking initiative typically includes raw and processed account data stored on back-end systems. In many cases, the data is "owned" by the end user, but stored on back-end systems under the custodial care of the business unit. The back-end system itself may be maintained by the IT department. The ownership definition aspect of the asset management policy should identify such relationships.

The change control aspects of asset management policy clearly establish the authority for modifying existing assets or introducing new ones. Similarly, the configuration management aspects establish the governance for setting up and maintaining approved configurations. Associated standards then would define these approved configurations. For example, METASeS has developed best practice configuration standards for Windows NT 4.0, UNIX, and other operating systems. These standards reside under the asset management policy in the METASeS Policy Framework.

Acceptable Use

The acceptable use policy addresses appropriate business use of the organization's assets. This includes items such as appropriately labeling, handling, and protection of corporate data and information. It also includes appropriate use of the organization's network and computing resources so that the information is not unnecessarily exposed – for example, through viruses or other malicious code that can be picked up by visiting illicit Web sites or by opening spurious e-mail.

Vulnerability Assessment and Management

Vulnerability assessment identifies and prioritizes an organization's technical, organizational, procedural, administrative, or physical security weaknesses. A vulnerability assessment should yield a traceable, prioritized "road map" for mitigating the assessed vulnerabilities. The vulnerability assessment and management policy provides governance for ongoing vulnerability management. Associated standards then define vulnerability assessment and management. For example, "internal vulnerability assessments shall be conducted monthly…", "the organization shall maintain metrics that allow comparison of current assessment results with results from the previous two assessments…", etc.

METASeS has found that most policy frameworks or documents do not explicitly address vulnerability assessment and management as a strategic Information Security topic. This is a direct result of the "challenge model" origin of such competing frameworks. (See the section How We Arrived at Our Framework above.) Yet vulnerabilities are clearly a central element of the risk equation, and assessment and management of vulnerabilities are essential policy topics.

Threat Assessment and Management

The threat assessment and management policy provides governance for threat assessment activities and ongoing threat management efforts. Associated standards then define these programs. For example, "threat assessments shall be conducted semi-annually…", "the organization shall maintain a capability to respond to, and contain, Denial of Service attacks against Category 1 assets within 30 minutes…", etc.

As with vulnerability assessment and management, METASeS has found that most policy frameworks and documents do not explicitly address threat assessment and management as a strategic topic. Again, this is a direct result of the "challenge model."

Standards and Procedures

The preceding discussion focused on the Information Security Charter and the six foundational policies: asset identification and classification; asset protection; asset management; acceptable use; vulnerability assessment and management; and threat assessment and management.

Each of the six policies has associated standards and procedures.

Standards define the acceptable level of security for a specific policy area. Standards may be technology- or solution-specific, and provide more measurable criteria for satisfying the high-level objectives defined in the policies. An operating system standard may state the requirements for hardening the operating system to provide adequate security. There may be one, or often more than one, standard for any given network element, depending on the different levels of security hardening required.

Procedures give specific, step-by-step advice on how to implement the various standards. For example, an NT configuration procedure would define, in detail, how to configure NT such that the system met the standard's requirements.

The threat assessment and monitoring policy has associated standards and procedures for threat assessment, incident response, etc.

Note that many other policy frameworks mention guidelines as integral elements of the policy framework document set. Figure 2-6 represents guidelines as the equivalent of standards that provide general direction prior to development of more definitive standards and procedures.

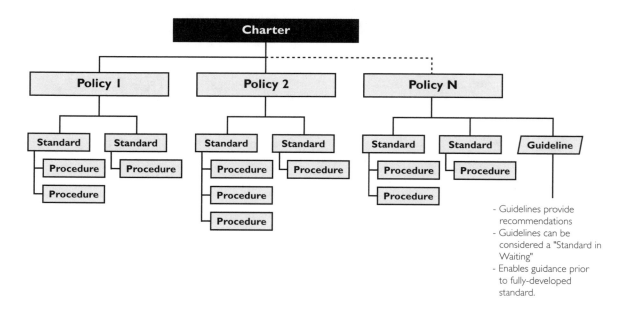

Figure 2-6: METASeS Best Practices Policy Framework -- Guidelines & Standards

In many cases, an organization may decide not to develop more definitive standards and procedures (due to, for example, resource or time constraints or immaturity of the associated technology), and rely solely on a guideline to provide further definition of the policy statements.

Policy Interpretation

The Best Practices Policy Framework satisfies the criteria for policy implementation. In particular, the six foundational policies are comprehensive in their coverage. With their associated standards and procedures, they provide a traceable progression from general governance objectives to detailed implementation procedures.

As noted above, the Framework should ensure minimal changes to top policy areas. It should be modular, allowing easy modification without necessitating a great many required changes. It should have the flexibility to handle swiftly changing technology without having to rewrite the policy all the time.

A central question is, "What happens to the policy arena when a new technology, such as one of revolutionary impact like the Internet, is introduced?" In other policy implementations, each fundamentally new application of technology results in a new top-level policy area (for example, Internet Acceptable Use Policy, or Remote Access Policy). Over time, such an approach leads to development of a complex, *ad hoc*, and cross-threaded policy framework. To avoid this outcome, the METASeS Framework provides for a dramatically different concept of policy interpretation.

Simply defined, policy interpretation is the application of existing policy guidance to a new IT or Information Security topic (see Figure 2-7).

Take, for example, wireless technologies, which hold great promise for eventually freeing users from static, "wired" links to routine, high-speed network access.[1] Using the Policy Framework, an organization might create a *Wireless Network Access Policy Interpretation* document. This concise document would concisely reference existing policy guidance and provide the basis for development of lower-level standards and procedures that apply to wireless technology.

To carry this example further, the *Wireless Network Access Policy Interpretation* document would simply reference the six foundational policies, as appropriate, and explain how they apply to the new technology. Then, new standards and procedures may be established too, for example:

- Define the organization's wireless network access protocol.

- Document steps to ensure appropriate protection of proprietary data during transmission.

- Establish a wireless vulnerability assessment standard that addresses such topics as determining the susceptibility of the organization's wireless signals to jamming.

The same approach could be applied to a new class of users. The Framework would help determine how to apply policies to a group of consultants, end users, or external firms, for example, who are beginning work for the organization. It could also help determine new standards and procedures for such personnel.

---

[1] Such a development goes well beyond the current situation in which hand-held devices (for example, some Palm Pilot models) may be used for relatively low-speed wireless access to networks. Currently, such devices are primarily for periodic network access and are generally regarded as unsuitable for use as full-service, heavy-duty network access devices.

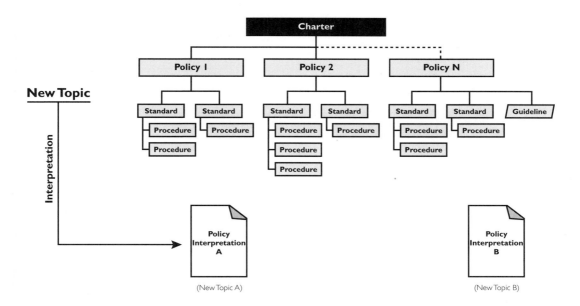

Figure 2-7: Policy Interpretation

The key advantage of the policy interpretation concept is that the organization does not have to revise or add top-level policies until the organization's fundamental Information Security objectives change. In practice, given the traceable development process for the Policy Framework, such change would have to be revolutionary enough to force strategic adjustments to fundamental risk management objectives.

Information Security Policy Life Cycle

Having discussed a framework for Information Security policy as well as policy interpretation, we'd like to turn now to the series of phases that constitutes a policy life cycle.

In our experience, an Information Security policy development and implementation effort can generally be divided into steps such as the following:

- Determining your policy
- Developing and revising the written policy document
- Implementing the policy
- Internalizing the policy
- Maintaining the policy

Your initial goal is to understand and document your organization's security needs so that you can craft the policy to appropriately reflect them. In this phase, you solicit input from staff members on what information assets have to be protected and what constitutes the threat. Determining your organization's risk profile and level of risk tolerance is critical, as these drive the scope and rigor of the policy. Attitudes and practices can vary widely within an organization and from one individual to another, so your assessment should extend to as broad a cross-section of the organization as possible.

Then you develop the policy document and have the appropriate parties within your organization review it.

Once senior management approves the policy, you begin the next step – implementation. Your activities should include formulating an approach for distributing the policy, setting up standards and procedures to support it, developing a training program, and establishing a mechanism, including auditing techniques such as intrusion detection, for enforcing compliance.

In a subsequent step, you should take action to institutionalize the policy as a normal mode of business operations. You will provide security awareness training for the entire user community, and gather feedback on its implementation. Finally, you want to maintain your policy – make required changes to it – over time.

The policy life cycle is an iterative process – your organization should plan to cycle through it biannually or annually, or every two years at most – to ensure that the policy and its supporting procedures and controls continue to meet your needs. The feedback you obtain provides input for subsequent cycles.

Assessing Policy Needs

This first phase of the policy development process is perhaps the most critical. Its purpose is to identify and categorize your information assets, evaluate the threats to them, assess vulnerabilities that may be exploited by the threats, and from this determine your organization's risk profile. The goal of an Information Security program is to manage risk, and to do that, you need to understand what your risks are.

Risk assessment identifies and prioritizes risks to guide an organization's appropriate application of safeguards. Risk assessment allows your organization to balance the value of assets at risk against the cost of risk mitigation, which includes the expense of security technologies and the inconvenience of security controls to internal users (employees), external users (customers and business partners), and system and network management staff. Risk is a measurement of how vulnerable a company is to existing threats. It is very important to understand that risk can never be completely eliminated; it can only be managed through the application of the right security measures. Companies, after all, are in business to make money and create value for owners and shareholders – not necessarily "to be secure." Thus, you need to treat security risks as you would any other business risk - and perform similar cost/benefit trade-offs. A risk assessment should yield a traceable, prioritized "road map" for mitigating the assessed risks.

The rigor and scope of your security policy and the cost of implementing it will be derived from the level of risk and your organization's level of risk tolerance. Risk tolerance is influenced by your type of business, corporate culture, the extent of outside regulation of business activities, and the level of trust which your customers and business partners place in the organization. The higher the level of risk, and the lower the level of risk tolerance, the more rigorous your security policy, standards, and procedures must be. The amount of resources you devote to security should be based on what your organization stands to lose, and on how well such a loss would be tolerated.

Once you carry out the the risk assessment process, you will have already done much of the up-front work in determining your policy requirements. You will have identified your critical information assets and business processes, the threats to the assets, and the risk that results. After you have made these basic determinations about the "what," you can begin to examine the "why" and the "how." You will want to conduct interviews with a cross-section of people in your organization, including the owners of key business processes, the guardians of information assets, legal counsel, and human resources. We recommend that you begin in Information Technology, especially the personnel in operations, development, and user support. These are the folks who have a vested interest in maintaining security and they may already have a good idea of needs to be done, or of what may not be getting done due to lack of resources, time, or skills!

You also should talk to the business owners of the applications or their designated custodians, depending on who is accountable for security. IT may not understand the business impact of the identified risks/threats.

In the interviews, you would ask questions like the following:

- How does the organization use IT to support its business mission?

- How are business decisions made?

- Who is included in or has input into the process?

- How is information about business decisions communicated?

- At what point in the process are requirements communicated?

- Is there a formal development or project life cycle?

- How are current Information Security efforts perceived in different groups in the organization?

- Do people from different parts of the organization perceive a gap between executive-level "vision" and day-to-day reality?

Drawing on the feedback from interviews, a security policy can be developed to give the organization an adequate level of protection while still enabling it to fulfill the business mission.

Reviewing Existing Policy

Your organization may have an existing information policy document, which should be reviewed to see if it is still up to date and needs refurbishing to reflect the organization's changed requirements. If the Information Security policy differs from existing practices, then current documents must either be updated or replaced. Instead of one omnibus document, you may have a collection of manuals, directives, policies, and forms that together comprise the *de facto* Information Security policy. In any case, you want to leverage prior initiatives to avoid reinventing the wheel. You also want to ensure that any new policy developed is consistent with existing directives, guidelines, and procedures. Conflicting statements in policy documents sow confusion among employees. Worse, they considerably complicate enforcement and weaken the organization's position in legal disputes.

There are two kinds of policy – explicit and implicit – and you should identify both when you start to review existing policy. Explicit policy is officially defined policy and should be fairly obvious to recognize. It will be formally marked as a policy, a directive, or a standard of behavior. Implicit policy is working policy that may not be formally documented or officially labeled as such. It can be trickier to ferret out. It could be expressed in service-level agreements with your customers or in supplier contracts. It may be contained in work practices, which may or may not be documented, or in departmental or divisional memos that have not been approved or implemented throughout the larger organization. The following are some examples of documents to look for:

- Computer policy handbook
- Remote access agreement form
- Acceptable use policy
- Internet access policy
- New employee and contract employee orientation materials
- Employee termination checklists
- Help desk guidelines
- Ethical standards
- Agreements with vendors and suppliers

If your company has been involved in a merger or acquisition, review of policy is particularly important. It will be necessary to bring everyone in the various organizations under the same policy umbrella. The faster that you can unify formerly disparate groups – who may in some cases have been competitors – and avoid having a motley patchwork of default policies, the better off you will be. Some companies actually perform a security and policy assessment as part of an acquisition. Hiring an objective consulting team to assess the target company's security posture, and performing a gap analysis against the acquiring company's policies, can produce a quick snapshot of the situation and a checklist for immediate action.

Overseas Considerations

Companies that have offices, subsidiaries, or partners outside the United States have additional considerations. There may be a different set of explicit and implicit policies for each country where you have a presence. These policies derive from local and regional law, as well as from regional values. In the European Union, privacy expectations will be based on the EU Directive on Data Protection, which is much more stringent than current U.S. practice. Hong Kong, Taiwan, and New Zealand also have stricter government regulation of privacy, while Australia and Japan follow the U.S. model, with its stress on self-regulation. In addition, employees in the EU enjoy a greater degree of job protection than in the U.S., where employment is typically "at will." Because of this, it is much harder to terminate an EU employee for a security violation, even with cause.

If you intend to put encryption on desktops, laptops, firewalls, or virtual private networks (VPNs) between offices in the US and abroad, you will need to take into account the latest U.S. regulations on the export of encryption technology. Regulation of encryption in other countries varies. France deregulated all use of encryption in 1999, while the People's Republic of China has banned the use of all non-PRC encryption tools and algorithms. Britain is trying to impose additional controls through the Regulation of Investigatory Powers Bill. Further information about U.S. encryption controls is available from the Electronic Privacy Information Center, at `www.epic.org`. UK and European Union information is available from the Foundation for Information Policy Research, at `www.fipr.org`.

Developing Information Security Policy

This section discusses some of the managerial aspects of developing Information Security policy.

Addressing Responsibility and Accountability

For policy development and implementation to succeed, someone must accept responsibility for it, and be held accountable for making it happen. The person in such a role is sometimes called the security policy "champion" – he or she "owns" the problem and drives the process. The champion should be sufficiently high up in the organization to have the authority to make critical decisions, adjudicate among disagreeing groups, and allocate resources – in other words, to possess the ability and authority to "make it happen."

All too often, however, the individual tasked with developing the security policy has the requisite technical knowledge, but lacks authority or political weight in the organization. This person may be able to produce a security policy document, but is typically unable to orchestrate its adoption and enforcement. You need a leader who has the authority and personality to make hard decisions and the clout to make them stick.

Information Security is an area where the authority accorded it often does not match its level of responsibility. System administrators and network managers hold the operational responsibility for making and keeping information assets secure. However, they are generally not given the authority to say "No" to managers and executives who may want to make unauthorized exceptions to the security policy. The war story below provides an example of this.

War Story:

We once conducted a pre-production security review of a new e-Commerce service offered by a very large, well-known company. During the process, we were in meetings that the company's internal auditors also attended. In a break room over coffee, they told us of a situation they had recently encountered in another division of the company. They had discovered that the LAN administrators had just installed a second 2 gigabyte (GB) disk on a senior vice president's desktop machine. (This was back in the days when 2 GB of memory were huge, and most desktops had a maximum of 800 megabytes (MB). Because this was unusual, they dug a little deeper and discovered that the VP had filled the entire first 2 GB with pornography downloaded from the Internet. The network administrators preferred continued employment to the dangers of confronting the senior executive over this issue, so they compromised. They would provide the VP with local disk space, as long as he kept the contraband files off their file servers. They figured they could add at least two additional disks before the man retired or was caught.

Many organizations would benefit from creating a dedicated, centralized security organization. The individual chosen to head this organization is likely the most appropriate candidate to "own" the policy. As such, this person would be responsible for the development of the policy and associated procedures and their implementation. Operational responsibility for the various tasks and activities would be delegated to staff. It is important to clearly define the delegation of these tasks to avoid gaps in coverage.

Who Should Formulate the Policy?

Who should actually formulate and write up the policy? For your security policy to be appropriate and effective, it must have acceptance and support from all levels of the organization. Much as in security program project design, you will need not only the backing of senior management, but also of the people who will actually implement the policy or who are most affected by it. When developing an organization-wide policy, you have to consider the differing perspectives of key functional areas and balance the desire for broad representation against efficiency of process. Therefore we recommend that you establish a security steering committee with representatives from across the organization.

A common reason policy efforts fail is that they are too often developed in a vacuum or by decree, and as a result do not reflect the security needs of the entire organization. Being inclusive from the start will make it easier to market the policy within the organization later.

The following questions should help identify the responsible parties to be directly involved in the policy life cycle:

- Who is responsible for the development of security policy?

- Who is responsible for the development of standards and procedures to implement the policy?

- Who is responsible for distributing the policy to employees and providing supporting security awareness training?

- Who is responsible for ensuring that policy and procedures are followed?

- Who is responsible for taking action if non-compliance is discovered?

- Who is responsible for ongoing maintenance of the policy?

- What resources are available to support these activities – staff, equipment, funding, etc.?

- Where does the development of security policy fit into the organizational infrastructure?

- How much support is there from senior management?

Figure 2-8 illustrates some of the individuals who should be involved in the creation and review of security policy documents.

This sampling is representative of many organizations, but is not necessarily comprehensive. The idea is to bring in representation from key stakeholders, management who have budget and policy authority, technical staff who know what can and cannot be supported, business staff who will be impacted, and legal counsel who know the legal ramifications of various policy choices. (The role of legal counsel will vary from country to country.) In some organizations, it may be appropriate to include audit personnel.

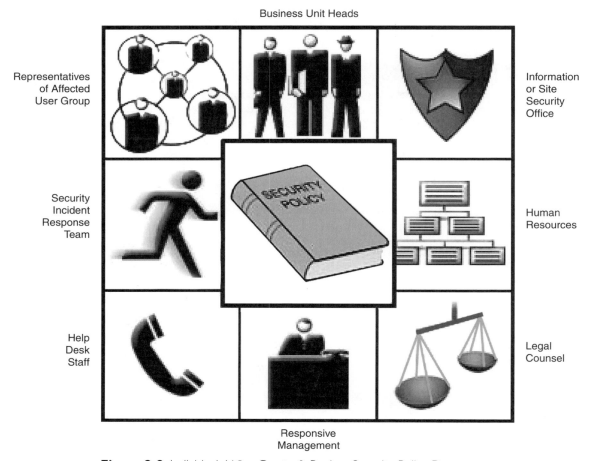

Figure 2-8: Individuals Who Create & Review Security Policy Documents

Accounting for Corporate Culture

The culture and management model of your organization will have a significant impact on the policy you develop and on the way that policy is received and implemented. In a traditional, top-down hierarchical management model, the lines of authority and the reporting structure should be fairly clear. This schema will ease development and implementation of the security policy. In a matrixed organization, on the other hand, the lines of authority and reporting structure are diffuse. From a security perspective, the problem with "matrix" management is that there are often no clearly defined responsible parties. The buck frequently stops with someone else and the responsible party depends on whom you ask! In such a situation, senior management has to make a special effort that there is explicitly defined accountability at all levels.

Organizations have varying levels of sensitivity to risk. The security policy must reflect your organization's particular areas of sensitivity to appropriately target security investments of people, money, and time. Two major factors drive an organization's level of risk sensitivity.

The first factor is the organization's ability to bear the consequences of a security incident, including the cost of recovery and restoration of services, the diversion of personnel for incident handling, the opportunity cost of business lost during downtime, and the threat to the organization's reputation and goodwill. Reliance on means of transferring risk, such as insurance or contractual instruments, may reduce the level of cost exposure so that the immediate dollar loss is not a major consideration.

The second factor is organizational or political sensitivity to risk. In some corporate cultures, the threat of an article in the national press highlighting an intrusion into their computer resources might be regarded as disastrous, even if the actual recovery costs are small. In open environments, such as universities and scientific research communities, management may feel that an occasional incident is more acceptable, and certainly more tolerable, than restricting the flow of information or access to outside resources. This attitude tends to result in conflict when scientists and academics move into the business world, in fields such as genetic research and pharmaceuticals, where huge sums of money and even entire business models are at stake.

Sensitivity to risk is not quite the same as *risk tolerance*, however, and both should be taken into account. Risk tolerance may be defined as the effect of organizational culture on sensitivity to risk. Brokerages and banks, for example, have similar sensitivity to risk: they are federally regulated, with stringent reporting requirements; they have custody of large amounts of their client's money; and they would both be adversely affected by a highly publicized security incident. But brokerages are much more risk-tolerant than general banks – brokers are, after all, people who engage in legal, high-stakes gambling for a living. (The trading culture of Wall Street is inherently more risk-taking, because the rewards for taking risks are higher and decisions must be immediately and continually made to take advantage of market upticks or downturns.)

In brief, security policy must be framed within the context of your organization's risk culture so that those affected will view it beneficially. This will require cooperation, creativity, and some really good internal marketing.

Managing Expectations

Good policy definition takes into account the organization's ability to affect change. Policies are often defined with no thought to their feasibility. They may be good in theory but are hamstrung in practice because of unrealistic expectations, technical ignorance, internal opposition, or insufficient resources for implementation.

Live Example:

Policy Statement (taken from an actual security policy):

"All powerful information systems tools that could be used to cause significant damage must be automatically restricted so that they can only be used for their intended purpose."

Reaction:

"Oops, guess we can't use 'em anymore!"

This is an example of a well-meaning but very narrow policy statement that is simply unenforceable. Policies need to be reality-checked before they are put into place.

It is important to set realistic expectations regarding the role policy plays within your organization. It must be realized that the security document itself cannot perform miracles. It cannot force an organization to make the often-difficult decisions to implement an appropriate level of security. You need to make a realistic assessment of your ability to impose standards and procedures that change ingrained user habits. For example, does your organization have the political will to reduce account privileges, when the actual need for those privileges does not match the user's perceived need? And what if, in such a case, the user is a senior vice president?

You have to make tough decisions and tradeoffs to provide an appropriate level of security that does not hinder business activities. Establishing a security policy will not necessarily make these issues easy, but it will help clarify and provide a framework for making the necessary decisions.

Further, you want to strike a balance between the benefits and costs of a particular policy or security control. For many companies that are launching e-Commerce projects, the most significant source of conflict lies between achieving the shortest "time to market," while at the same time performing security analyses to ensure the security of products and services before they go "live." Yet an organization can take several actions to reduce the restrictive impact security might have on the service development process. These include the following:

- Considering security issues early in the development process

- Limiting the number of products and services to those which can be securely delivered with current resources

- Or, simply, assigning additional resources.

Unfortunately, the natural inclination of many business unit managers is to avoid making a hard decision by making the security information policy as weak as possible.

You can expect that other conflicts will arise with respect to ease of use versus good security practices. There will be times when you will need to distinguish between what is simply current practice and what is a true security need. Some security controls will be perceived as too restrictive to be implemented. A decision not to implement may be quite appropriate, as long as it has been carefully thought out and there is a clear understanding of the residual risk. When such conflicts arise and you have to negotiate tradeoffs, keep your policy goals in mind. If, for example, you are relying on the policy to reduce your organization's liability, it must at least prescribe a level of security considered reasonable within your industry.

Exception Handling

It is not realistic to expect that a policy always adequately addresses every contingency. Sometimes valid business requirements conflict with policy, and undoubtedly the policy or supporting procedures will not anticipate certain requirements. There is always a need for appropriate handling of policy exceptions, so it is important that the policy include provisions for conflict resolution.

Some organizations handle this through a proposal or request process whereby the business unit desiring the exception submits a request with supporting documentation. The request package should answer the following questions:

- What is the requested exception?

- Why is it necessary, that is, what is the business need?

- What is the level of risk?

- What benefits will accrue from the exception to offset the risk?

A senior executive or a steering committee, after reviewing the cost/benefit analysis, then makes the decision. Committee review may take longer, but may be less subject to pressures for individual career advancement or favoritism. Further, there must be someone in the organization who is explicitly authorized to accept and take responsibility for any added risk. An additional step in the review process could be the technical review of the request, to provide added input on the risk and generate suggestions for risk mitigation. Approval could be contingent on the use of alternative technology, improved monitoring, etc.

This review process shouldn't be limited to policy exceptions – we recommend that you go through a similar evaluation and analysis any time you plan to introduce a new technology or a major network component, such as a new Web-based customer database or a Web storefront. You should develop guidelines for your business units to follow for new development or acquisition projects so that they receive a security review right from inception. (Not three weeks before the $5 million, six-month project is supposed to go live!)

Implementing and Deploying Policy

The changes resulting from the definition and implementation of an Information Security policy can be dramatic. The way in which you chose to deploy your new policy can make or break its acceptance and practical effectiveness.

We've stressed repeatedly how important the visible support of management is to the success of the policy effort. Support takes many forms, and executives who are good leaders encourage their staff to comply through the power of their own personal example, that is, their commitment to "walk the talk." But that personal commitment must also translate to more tangible support, including provision of adequate human resources and funding. Both are required, in most cases, to bring existing architecture and practices into conformance with the policy.

A smart organization assesses the requirements for this and then creates a plan to implement the changes in phases. This ensures that operations aren't seriously impacted and that staff is not overwhelmed by too much change at one time. The deployment plan outlines steps for the distribution of the policy, the training that should accompany it, the creation of supporting procedures and practices, and the assignment of specific responsibilities for those tasks.

Users cannot be expected to comply with the policy until they are given the tools to do so. As a rule of thumb, for every objective the policy document identifies, a clear means must exist for meeting it. This involves both creating new procedures and practices, as well as modifying some existing ones. Not all procedures and practices will target the user community; for example, you will also need to create or update procedures and guidelines for the administrators of firewalls, routers, and other network devices, as well as servers and desktop systems.

The policy should be as well-advertised and as widely available as possible, with rollout combined with awareness training (see the following section). Users should have easy access to copies of the complete policy, which may mean distributing one physical copy per person, or one per department combined with Web-based intranet access. Putting the document on-line with a user-friendly interface and a good indexing or search tool encourages users to regularly refer to it.

While access to the full policy is important, it is often helpful to provide non-technical end users with an additional handout that concisely identifies the fundamental policy points which apply directly to them. This is called an end user policy. The handout can be small and printed on laminated card stock and can be kept on desktops or bulletin boards as a constant reminder of policy. It should summarize the policy expectations for users and management, and pair that with information specifically directed to personal or desktop user security. This might include information about choosing safe passwords, checking for viruses, backing up files, and securing floppy disks. This pocket "user guide" should also provide information on where to go for help or to report problems, where to find additional information, and who to contact with questions or suggestions.

War Story

The policy needs to be made available to everyone in the organization. We once helped run a pre-deployment meeting for a client about to roll out his newly minted security policy. One senior executive pushed very hard to keep the complete policy out of the end users' hands, on the grounds that they didn't need to be bothered with the sections that applied only to managers – it would only confuse them, he said. It quickly became apparent that he did not want his own staff to know what his responsibilities were under the new policy! Fortunately, his colleagues quickly shot down this idea.

Awareness and Education

The successful implementation of the security policy depends on the actions, knowledge, and discretion of the user population, so it is critical the distribution of the policy be accompanied by security awareness training. Users are more likely to comply with a policy when they understand what's really at risk. You don't want them viewing it as an arbitrary set of obstacles to getting work done.

When the policy is distributed, you should conduct awareness training for all segments of the user population to ensure that users understand their responsibilities and the reasoning behind them. It should also be incorporated into all new hire and contractor training, and recapped in annual refresher sessions, or whatever timeframe is feasible.

The most important training goal should be to help users recognize their responsibility in protecting the company's data assets. Many users don't view the data on their desktop PC or local server as something with a real dollar value. Nor do they see it as a corporate asset that belongs to the company. They may regard it as "their" data. Yet if users know it is wrong to take sensitive printouts out of the building, they should have the same attitude about electronic data. Users need to understand that an attacker can employ even innocuous-seeming information to build a profile of the organization for launching an electronic offensive.

You may want to stage demos to show users how their actions can put the entire organization at risk, and what steps they should take if they become aware of potential threats or unusual activities. You may even want to orchestrate role playing activities to demonstrate how outsiders, posing as legitimate employees or contractors, can exploit naïve users for vital information. Further, users who are new to the Internet environment need to be warned about spam, e-mail viruses, and destructive chain letters.

Urban Legends and Web Chain Letters

"Urban legends," Internet chain letters, and virus hoaxes are the bane of system and network administrators everywhere. Urban legends are cautionary folk stories which are often claimed to be true, having happened to "a friend of a friend." Internet chain letters and virus hoaxes are the modern form of urban legend for the digital age, able to be propagated to a large number of recipients with one mouse click. They often admonish the reader to "Distribute this letter to as many people as possible," and do not list the name and contact information of the original sender, which any legitimate warning or solicitation would do.

Chain letters and hoaxes can damage reputations, as well as clog networks. The American Cancer Society has been the victim of several chain letters which claimed that it would donate money for every time the chain letter was passed along. Chain letters and hoaxes often prey on our fears, like the ones which claim that children have died of poisonous snake or spider bites in the play areas of fast-food restaurants, or that evil drug dealers are hooking innocent school children with LSD-laden "Blue Star Tattoos," or even that imported bananas carry flesh-eating bacteria. Sometimes they pander to greed, such as the ones that claim that Bill Gates will pay users to beta-test Microsoft software, or that Disney is giving away free vacations.

Teach your users how to recognize hoaxes and legends, and instruct them that if they receive a chain letter, to either delete it or send it to the local Information Security officer or system administrator. By no means should they pass it along to the entire company, their friends and relatives, or mailing lists to which they subscribe.

More information on urban legends, hoaxes and chain letters can be found at www.snopes2.com (The San Fernando Valley Folklore Society) and www.ciac.org/ciac (the Computer Incident Alert Capability site of the US Department of Energy).

Remember that awareness training is also a marketing tool to help you sell security policy. You want to present your efforts in ways that win user acceptance and buy into the principles on which it is based. Evangelize the security message: Focus on the positive aspects of security and the benefits to the company and the user, and don't forget to make it fun whenever you can. Supplement periodic training sessions, on an ongoing basis, with other types of awareness reinforcement – including e-mail reminders, articles in organization newsletters, contests, logon banners, posters, and handouts. Some companies might even use comic books.

If new software tools are required for compliance, be sure that users are well trained in their use. Desktop security tools are notoriously counter-intuitive. A team of researchers from Carnegie Mellon University and the University of California at Berkeley has been studying the usability of security tools for the average non-technical user.[2] Their starting premise was that user errors cause or contribute to most security failures. The researchers found that user interfaces for security products tend to be clumsy, confusing, or non-existent. So, until software development houses see the light, you must spend time in training users and in pre-configuring software to improve their usability. This will encourage users to make greater use of these important tools.

Compliance and Enforcement

A policy that is not consistently enforced is worse than having no policy at all. It will quickly engender contempt and be honored more in the breach than in the practice. You need to establish processes for measuring compliance, detecting non-compliance, and responding to violations of your policy. These processes are necessary to make sure that users are held accountable for their actions, as well as to guard against the consequences of inappropriate actions.

The processes you establish should include periodic reviews of network architecture, host and server configurations, adherence to mandated practices and procedures, and business requirements. In addition to regular reviews, you need to decide what type and level of ongoing monitoring you will employ, including usage logging, password checking tools, and intrusion detection.

Most organizations prefer positive reinforcement to negative enforcement — few managers enjoy writing incident reports or terminating employees. You want to make it as easy as possible for people to comply with the policy through education and the appropriate use of tools and technology. However, you must also be prepared to deal with non-compliance by establishing penalties in advance and implementing them consistently. This is one area in particular where you want to have legal counsel and representatives from human resources involved in developing the policy and supporting procedures. You also need to ensure that all affected parties are fully informed on what constitutes a violation, the associated schedule of penalties and remedies, and how you monitor for non-compliance.

You want to adhere to your security incident response plan, which is the set of detailed procedures that follow through on the principles outlined in your policy. Internal security incidents that do not involve misuse of organizational resources may well be the result of ignorance and your policy needs to take that into consideration. You never want to discourage staff from reporting information that may be evidence of a breach, or that could

---

[2] Witten, Alma and Tygar, J.D., "Why Johnny Can't Encrypt: A Usability Evaluation of PGP 5.0", Proceedings of the Eighth USENIX Security Symposium, August 1999.

be used constructively to prevent future incidents. In addition, establish guidelines on the liability of personnel in the event of a security breach. It is important to be sure what role a staff member may have played in a breach. You might specify different administrative actions for violations that resulted from ignorance or lack of training, as opposed to intentional intrusions or misuse. We should note, of course, that the better job you do writing and disseminating your policy and educating your users, the less likely anyone on your staff can claim ignorance, for example, that she had "no idea" she was not allowed to run password sniffing tools on the LAN without permission!

War Story

A few years ago, we were teaching a class for Information Security staff at a large pharmaceutical house when the corporate director of security mentioned that he would have to slip out for a while later that afternoon. He was going to participate in the termination of an employee who had been caught downloading pornography from the Internet. It was, he said, the fourth such termination that year, but he hoped it would also be the last. The first three had been kept quiet, but this one would be different in that he intended to make it widely known that the company would follow through on any policy violation. We agreed that public executions were a wonderful way to focus the staff's attention on an issue. Today, this reaction is becoming more and more commonplace. In October of 1999, Xerox Corporation announced that it had terminated at least 40 employees so far that year for inappropriate use of Internet resources.

Maintaining Information Security Policy

Once a security policy is implemented and promulgated throughout the organization, it must be maintained. In the area of maintenance, it is important once again to distinguish between policy and procedures. Policy should be sufficiently strategic in scope to avoid having to make frequent minor changes in security practice. Even so, policies do require regular review and tuning, especially after they are first put into effect.

A mechanism for review should be built into the policy itself. During the first year of implementation, and perhaps even quarterly, you want to conduct frequent reviews. Thereafter, an annual review should suffice. You may also want to anticipate the need for additional reviews contingent on special circumstances – such as a merger or acquisition, a major architectural change, or a serious security incident.

When reviewing policy, consider questions like the following:

- How has the policy been received?

- What is the rate of compliance and in what ways have you measured compliance?

- How easy or difficult has it been for users to comply with the policy?

- Have any sections of the policy proven to be unrealistic in actual practice?

- Have there been an inordinate number of exception requests?

- Have there been new security incidents in the company or industry which would cause you to re-examine your level of risk or other assumptions on which the policy is based?

- Has there been new legislation, regulation, or a change in the legal climate which requires a policy response?

- Has your organization changed significantly since the last review – through rapid growth, an initial public offering, large government contracts, unionization, etc.?

Remember, security is a way of life, not a one-time commodity – you can't go out to the convenience store to pick up two quarts of milk and a loaf of security. As with brushing your teeth, you have to do it every day, even several times a day. Use the lessons from every phase of your policy development and implementation life cycle to make the next phase even better, and don't ever stop evolving progressively better solutions.

Web and e-Commerce Security:
Architecture, Life Cycle Development and Infrastructure

3

Thus far, our focus has been on the overarching security program, rather than specific Web or Internet technologies. In this chapter, we address the key elements of building secure Web and e-Commerce systems. This chapter is one part definition, one part security architecture, one part process, and one part infrastructure. Specifically, we discuss Information Security goals, security architecture, making security an integral part of the system development life cycle (SDLC), and infrastructure components such as firewalls and virus scanning. Our intent is to provide you with the fundamental tools – basic business and technical understanding, sample architectures, and processes – for successfully building a secure Web or e-Commerce architecture. We will both "teach you how to fish" and we will "give you fish."

Do not expect this chapter to cover each and every security technology, security consideration, or e-Commerce architecture permutation, or to turn you instantly into a top-flight security architect. After all, developing a secure architecture for a Web or e-Commerce system always requires a team effort that balances security concerns with other business and operational requirements. Our intent is to provide practical guidance on meeting the unique business, operational, and technical objectives of a system.

Some would argue that this chapter's discussion of architecture and security technology is the real meat of the report, and that the reader should jump straight to it while ignoring the higher-level issues in chapters 1 and 2. While reading ahead is fine – especially to satiate a technical appetite – you should remember that Web and e-Commerce security have a hierarchy. First, policy, then program, and only then, architecture. Even if your organization could develop perfect technical security architectures, it would remain at risk – potentially significant risk – if it did not adequately address the other program and Information Security policy areas.

For example, perfect security architecture does not prevent end users from writing down their passwords and posting them for all to see on their monitors – a practice we affectionately refer to as the Yellow Sticky password problem. Perfect architecture also doesn't thwart an attacker using "social engineering techniques" – like a phone call from an intruder posing as a security administrator – to obtain unauthorized access. Finally, even the best network security architecture cannot ensure that employees will avoid dumb actions such as installing modems inside a firewall on internal network segments, thus allowing crackers to sail on into the system. As discussed in chapters 1 and 2, good security requires a solid security program, replete with policies, standards, procedures, processes, and the requisite training and motivational overtures. Clear policies, a solid and prolonged security awareness program, and the appropriate motivations (for example, infusing security objectives in employee appraisals and providing rewards for participation) are, together with solid architecture, the way to deal with security.

Unfortunately, in the real world where things are moving at Internet speed, you often don't have time or resources to address all of the security program elements first. Expending the considerable effort required to bring the entire program up to snuff before dealing with the horde of new Web and e-Commerce applications is a luxury many organizations simply don't have. Asking the business groups to defer for a year or so new Web-based applications – applications that will help improve their competitiveness and boost their bonuses and salaries – is rarely an option. Thus, most organizations are forced to tackle high-priority program components while simultaneously spending a significant time to design and deploy secure Web or e-Commerce applications and infrastructure. Overwhelmed organizations may have to turn to the experts for advice. (We admit that the current business environment is akin to a Security Consultant Full Employment Act and bodes well for those of us in the security business!)

Chapter Components

This chapter examines the best practices for framing a secure environment for Web/e-Commerce projects. We cover four major topics:

1. Information Security Goals – Defining exactly what the security architecture is attempting to accomplish.

2. Security Architecture and Design for Web and e-Commerce systems – Process for planning and assembling the various technical and non-technical elements of a system to meet the security goals.

3. System Development Life Cycle – Guidance on the phases for building a specific Web/e-Commerce project, and how to incorporate the appropriate security solutions.

4. Underlying Infrastructure Components – Defining the basic technical elements of e-Commerce and network security, such as Web servers and firewalls. We also discuss some specific, component-level security vulnerabilities and mitigation recommendations for achieving the security goals.

Information Security Goals

Security architecture – and the various technical and non-technical security controls that underpin it – is a set of mechanisms to accomplish the business and security goals. It is necessary to first understand the goals driving the architecture.

From an Information Security perspective, there is a short list of fundamental security goals. Based on an exhaustive review of this area, we adapted Donn B. Parker's list of goals from his classic 1998 work *Fighting Computer Crime: A New Framework For Protecting Information*. In his book, Parker updates the traditional "CIA" list – Confidentially, Integrity, Availability – to reflect a more comprehensive set of goals that a security architecture needs to address. We added two considerations of our own that are important in the Internet arena.

In his work, the "Donn of Security" highlights the three primary security goals, organized into six elements[1] :

- **Confidentiality and Possession** – Maintaining the secrecy and control of information whether it is traversing a network, or maintained on a workstation, server, or in paper form.

- **Integrity and Authenticity** – Ensuring the completeness and validity of information.

- **Availability and Utility** – Ensuring the usability and usefulness of information and the systems it resides on or is accessed through.

As Parker states: "…to adequately eliminate (or at least reduce) security threats, all six elements need to be considered to ensure that nothing is overlooked in applying appropriate controls. These elements are also useful for identifying and anticipating the types of abusive actions that adversaries may take – before such actions are undertaken."

These items make up the fundamental goals that architecture teams need to consider prior to developing a security solution. The solution includes not only technical controls defined in a technical architecture and enumerated in a system design, but also non-technical controls defined in a set of processes and procedures.

In addition to Parker's six elements, we include two other elements to address in Web or e-Commerce applications. They are as follows:

- **Non-repudiation**[2] – The ability to ensure that parties in a transaction cannot deny (repudiate) that the transaction took place.

- **Auditability**[3] - The ability to track user or system activity for future reference or through real-time monitoring and logging.

---

[1] Parker actually separates his list into six different goals, but later in the book abbreviates the related elements.

[2] Parker accurately argues that non-repudiation does not encompass all the various ways "information can be misrepresented." However, since business transactions are a key component of e-Commerce, we believe non-repudiation is useful as a key architectural goal.

[3] While auditability is not necessarily a fundamental "goal." we believe it is at least a key architectural consideration, given the need to provide due care to investigate security breaches.

One of the most important aspects of architecture in general, and security architecture specifically, is the ability to trace architecture back to clear business goals. This is not unlike building a house, where a good homebuilder first spends a significant amount of time trying to understand the customer's requirements according to broad categories. For example, he would consider space requirements based on the size of the family, or stylistic requirements based on a preference for a contemporary or a more traditional home, etc., before making more specific design decisions like the size or type of rooms. In a similar way, the basic security goals provide direction for the security architecture.

Figure 3-1 shows the fundamental security goals and some of the methods and tools used to satisfy the goals.

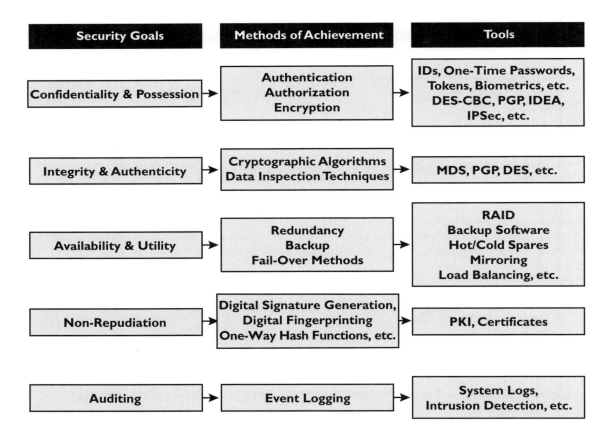

Figure 3-1: Security Goals, Methods, & Tools

One of the easiest ways to lead business application or data owners through the security requirements discussion is to ask questions about the information being protected and the relative importance of each of the security goals – without delving into the technical details (methods, technologies, tools, etc.). Eventually the discussion needs to address some of the detailed, technical procedural control items, but the initial discussions are more productive if they remain at a higher level. To use the homebuilding analogy again, the builder would consider the bathroom fixtures or kitchen appliances only after understanding the size of the rooms.

We have taken part in many security architecture discussions where the IT team focused on low-level technical design decisions with the business application/data owners. The result was that the security goals became mixed up with a discussion of technology and methods.

If the fundamental goals are never clearly understood, especially by the information owners, nor balanced with cost and risk considerations, the solution will likely not achieve the goals within budget constraints. Further, if the discussions with the business owners are down at the "geek speak" level, it becomes nearly impossible to guide the business team toward the key issues that can lead to an appropriate solution. More importantly, the IT team will likely lose significant credibility with the application/information owners from the business side. More than once our consultants have had to field phone calls from business folks who were "fed up dealing with the IT or security team," and sought someone to bridge the gaping business and technical divide. We are aware of numerous projects that have gone awry because of these matters.

The main security goals are discussed in the sections that follow.

Confidentiality and Possession

Organizations invest time and resources to research and develop products, collect information, or create other intellectual capital. In many cases, the intellectual capital is the nucleus of the business, and the organization's competitive advantage. In addition, many organizations are in custodial care of partner or customer information that needs to be protected. Confidentiality is the goal of keeping this type of information private. Confidentiality can be undercut by observation of the data, deliberate or not, and whether the data in question is disclosed or not.

Possession involves data that a user owns but is not necessarily aware of. This is especially true in an increasingly computerized world with massive amounts of information, with which a user cannot possibly hope to be thoroughly familiar.

The chief methods for achieving confidentiality and possession are as follows:

- **Authentication** – Provides the means for identifying systems or people through the proper credentials. Once authenticated, user actions can be audited. Tools include simple ID/password combinations, software or hardware tokens, two-way authentication, and biometrics.

- **Authorization** – Used in parallel with authentication to protect system or network resources. The authorization process uses the information that has been captured by the authentication process, such as user ID, group, and domain, to allow access to resources based on permissions and rights granted to the user or application. The tools that can facilitate authorization may be a collaboration of authentication and system tools. For example, the authorization process inspects the permissions or rights that a user has over a resource based on the credentials presented upon authentication.

- **Encryption** – Helps to protect data transmitted across a network or stored locally on a machine by scrambling it. It can normally only be decrypted (unscrambled) by the intended recipient or owner. In addition, in support of confidentiality, encryption ensures that credentials or personal and system identification information (keys, passwords, addresses, etc.) used to authenticate and authorize a person or system cannot be compromised. Tools include encryption algorithms such as triple DES (Data Encryption Standard) or protocols such as IPSec.

Integrity and Authenticity

Integrity refers to the consistency of the data. This goal specifically relates to the need to ensure that an unauthorized person or system cannot inadvertently or intentionally alter data without the modification being detected. Examples are a database of pricing information where the data could be altered for the financial advantage of the perpetrator, or a financial report on a Web site that was intentionally altered for stock market advantage.

Authenticity refers to the ability to know that the information accessed is genuine. An example of a breach of authenticity would be a perpetrator falsely posting an official-looking company press release in a public place like a news portal. Authenticity controls include transaction confirmation, product validation, and range checking.

In an e-Commerce environment, integrity is a critical factor in the validity of the data being exchanged and stored. To ensure data integrity, cryptographic algorithms and data inspection techniques are used. Tools such as cryptographic hash functions (for example, MD5), in combination with sound programming techniques for data inspection, also may be employed. Digital signatures can help ensure the authenticity of information.

Availability and Utility

Availability refers to the accessibility and usability of information. It is essential for an e-Commerce provider to incorporate availability in the initial design and deployment of the network. Imagine the customer dissatisfaction and loss of revenue of an on-line store if it were disrupted from servicing customer orders during the Christmas season — especially where the Internet places the customer only a few mouse clicks away from a competitor.

Utility refers to how useful information is. For example, if the encryption key to data were erased by accident, the usefulness of the information would be lost. (Even though its confidentiality would increase!)

Methods for achieving availability include backup of data, redundancy, and fail-over methods that provide service continuity. The tools for achieving availability include the following:

- Local or network backup systems
- *Cold* or *hot* stand-by equipment that can be swapped or automatically activated to start processing information
- Mirroring that allows data to be available in physically separate locations, thus minimizing the risk of single point of failure
- Load balancing techniques that help minimize the risk for potential system failure

Utility can be achieved by maintaining backup copies of information and of the various keys used to encrypt them.

Auditibility

It is necessary to generate and keep historical records of events such as authentication, resource access, and data exchanges. These records can help detect inappropriate use of resources or signs of intrusion. They must be handled with the proper care (for example, digitally signed, encrypted and stored in a safe place) to be admissible in court, in the event they are used to prosecute someone who steals or damages your data.

Event logging is a method for recording historical data. Typically, computer systems are configured by default to record general events such as operational errors, access requests, failures, or successful logins. Although this provides some accounting capabilities, it may not provide the required level of detail to recreate a clear picture of events. A system that maintains customer information may be configured to record only general events such as program errors or run-time library errors.

The proper way to configure the system to log events is to first evaluate the purpose of the system and the data that is maintained. Then, on a system where sensitive customer information is kept, you should record the appropriate events so that a complete, detailed picture of a user's session can be reconstructed. Some of the events to be logged include, but are not limited to, login successes/failures, access rights successes/failures, remote connection requests, or resource access. Tools that provide event logging include operating system logging mechanisms and intrusion detection systems.

Non-Repudiation

Non-repudiation provides evidence for verifying the identity of a person engaged in a business transaction, such that he cannot deny being a party to the transaction. In the non-digital world, this is typically accomplished through a signature and, in certain instances, backed up by a third-party witness such as a notary public.

A typical instance of non-repudiation involves a person sending a message and the recipient having to verify that the originator is the author of the message. Further, the originator must not be able to deny ownership of the message. For example, in the event of a dispute with a customer, an on-line brokerage firm must be able to prove in court that transactions submitted to purchase or sell stock are authentic and came from the person in question.

Cryptographic methods such as generating digital signatures or digital fingerprinting help implement non-repudiation. However, while digital signatures can provide non-repudiation from a technical standpoint, non-repudiation is not guaranteed in all circumstances. For example, compromise of a user's private key, the existence of a user's private key on a set of corporate backup tapes, a virus infection, or malfunctioning software can all cast significant doubt upon whether the human owner of a digital signature was actually responsible for the signature.

Importance of Goals

The goals of confidentiality and possession, integrity and authenticity, availability and utility, auditing, and non-repudiation must be incorporated into the process of building and maintaining any computer network, especially networks that provide e-Commerce services prone to attack. They are the fundamental business requirements of the security architecture. Moreover, down at the network component level, a particular goal may be emphasized more than others, based on the function of the respective network components. For example, a component such as a firewall will require stronger authentication, more detailed accounting, and greater availability than an anonymous FTP server or a message board. This is discussed in more detail in the section Underlying Infrastructure Components.

Understanding these fundamental security goals helps the organization formulate a sound solution for protecting its information assets. It is one of the most important inputs to the next step for enhancing your security environment – defining an appropriately secure architecture.

Web and e-Commerce Security Architecture

This section discusses how to formulate security architecture and outlines the different types of architecture.

Definition

Architecture means many things to many people. For us, architecture is a set of principles or a road map that guides the engineering process and product selection and includes detailed design, product selection, construction, implementation, support, and management of an organization's information systems and technology infrastructure.[4] Architecture is not simply an approved product list or a network diagram.

An architecture can be formulated at multiple levels. For example, an organization can define an enterprise-wide architecture that guides all development activities, as well as information systems and infrastructure development activities such as networks, servers, and middleware (Figure 3-2).

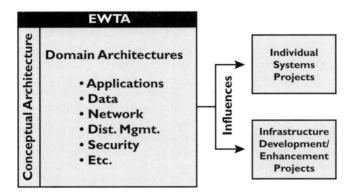

Enterprise-Wide Technical Architecture (EWTA) is a logicaly consistent set of principles that:
- Are derived from business requirements
- Guide the engineering of an organization's information systems and technology infrastructure across the various domain architectures
- Are understood and supported by senior corporate management and business units
- Take into account the full context in which the EWTA will be applied
- Enable rapid change in a company's business processes and the applications that enable them

Figure 3-2: Enterprise-Wide Technical Architecture (EWTA)

An enterprise-wide architecture helps steer projects towards a desired future state. In this context, architecture enables organizations to develop systems that meet business goals and objectives over a period of time.

---

[4] Source: META Group, "Enterprise Architecture Strategies"

Architecture also can refer more specifically to a subnetwork or a specific business system. Such a system-level architecture typically includes a more specific set of goals and requirements that drive the system design. We refer to system-level security architecture as it applies to a specific business system project (see Figure 3-3). We focus only on the Information Security aspects of the system-level security architecture. These are technical and non-technical controls to achieve the business security goals. In this section, we will spend the majority of time discussing the technical control mechanisms.

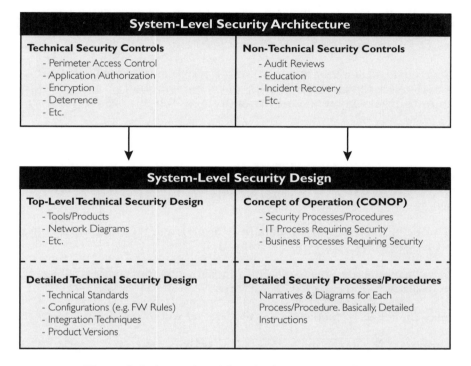

Figure 3-3: System-Level Security Architecture & Design

The intersection of the fundamental security goals discussed above, and the various types of e-business applications, provide the context for discussing security architecture. Architecture in this light is the manifestation of business goals in a set of supporting "systems." These systems include both technical elements – for example, access control mechanisms[5] or authentication servers – as well as various non-technical processes and procedures – for example dual entry, auditing, or division of responsibilities. Each of the different types of business uses of the Web has different security requirements or goals, and different organizations will necessarily prioritize these differently, based on their unique requirements and risk tolerances.

The line between architecture and system design is often blurry. In its pure form, which is rarely encountered "in the wild," architecture is expressed as a set of goals or requirements.

---

[5] Access controls are a collection of mechanisms that regulate access by entities (individuals, programs, processes, systems) to resources (data, systems, hardware, and software). Access is based on the security policy objectives (such as data confidentiality) of a given system or organization. The goal of access control is to prevent the unauthorized use of resources or the unauthorized disclosure or modification of data. Access control has two principal elements: authorization and authentication.

Design, on the other hand, is the expression of logical and physical configurations for the technical components required to achieve the goals. Further, on the non-technical side, design gets into the definition of the specific tasks or steps for processes and procedures. Information Security architecture, for example, may express the goal of restricting perimeter network access, but would not necessarily mandate a specific firewall, which might fall under design's purview.

Academic musing about the split between architecture and design is not important. What is critical is that you express the architecture at some level in terms of specific goals or requirements. This provides the key linkage to the business objectives.

The Process of Formulating Architecture

Formulating system-level security architecture is a process with inputs and outputs.   Below we illustrate both the traditional architecture development process, and a "fast path" method for meeting the stringent time requirements of the new Web business world.

Figure 3-4 depicts the traditional process flow for developing a system-level security architecture.

The fundamental security goals are one of the main inputs to the system-level security architecture of a Web or e-Commerce business system. Other key inputs to the system-level security architecture include the following:

- **Assets** – The nature and value of data or information to be protected by the security sub-architecture and other non-technical controls.

- **Threats** – Characterization of would-be attackers, and the misuse or abuse that they are likely to purposely or accidentally perpetrate.

- **Activities** – Malicious or inadvertent activities that would negatively impact the business.

- **Consequences** – The impact on business if an activity resulted in a security breach.

- **Current and Future Business Goals** – What the business system and information owners want to achieve with the system today and in the future. By considering future business requirements during the architecture and design process, the security team will not lock itself into a design that meets only current considerations.

- **External Regulatory Requirements and Corporate Information Security Policy** – What external and internal requirements must be addressed. For example:

  - *Health Care* – HIPAA (Health Insurance Portability and Accountability Act)
  - *Banking Finance* – OCC (Office of the Comptroller of the Currency of the U.S. Treasury)
  - *Commercial Entities* – SEC (Securities and Exchange Commission)
  - *Government Contractors* – Department of Defense (DoD) requirements such as evaluation against common criteria
  - *Basic Due Care Considerations for All Organizations* (refer to the following text box)

"Due Diligence" and Sentencing Guidelines

In regards to regulatory requirements and security, it is interesting to take note of the Federal Sentencing Guidelines for Criminal Conviction. These define executive responsibility for fraud, theft, and anti-trust violations, and establish a mandatory point system for Federal judges to determine appropriate punishment. Since much fraud and falsification of corporate data involves access to computer-held data, liability established under the Guidelines extend to computer-related crime. The mandatory punishment could apply when either intruders or insiders enter a computer system and perpetrate a crime.

While the Guidelines have a mandatory scoring system for punishment, they also have an incentive for proactive crime prevention. The requirement is for management to show "due diligence" in establishing an effective compliance program. There are seven elements that capture the basic functions inherent in most compliance programs:

1. Establish policies, standards, and procedures to guide the workforce.
2. Appoint a high-level manager to oversee compliance with the policy, standards and procedures.
3. Exercise due care when granting discretionary authority to employees.
4. Assure compliance policies are carried out.
5. Communicate the standards and procedures to all employees and others.
6. Enforce the policies, standards and procedures consistently through appropriate disciplinary measures.
7. Implement procedures for corrections and modifications in case of violations.

Before attempting to define technical and non-technical control requirements, it is critically important to know what needs to be protected (assets), what they need to be protected from (threat, activities), and what the resulting business consequences would be if the protective measures are not taken or prove inadequate. For commercial businesses, there are many consequences, all funneling down to either revenue impact or profit impact or both. In the non-commercial world, a major consequence is the loss of reputation or trust from employees, customers, or constituents.

One key input that is often overlooked, or given too little attention, is threat. In some situations, the threat is small enough to warrant no security controls at all! Be careful, however – it is possible that several apparently insignificant threats could create a large vulnerability. It is also important to understand the value of the assets being protected so that the budget for the security solution is in line with both it and the potential threat. The output is a set of goals or principles that meets the information protection requirements of the business.

Armed with these first-order considerations, the architecture team can lead the business team through facilitated discussions. Much of the "input" information will be sketchy or unknown prior to the facilitated sessions on security. Thus, these sessions should fill in the details, or correct the assumptions of the architecture team. Preparing for the facilitated sessions with a first cut of the input assumptions and a set of questions to clarify the inputs is important.

Given the very diverse information needed to establish the architecture – from threat information to business operations and technical considerations – multiple sessions are likely necessary. Alternatively, at a minimum, a single session is required with representation from various groups (for example, the business owner, business middle management, applications development, IT architecture and operations). We recommend splitting the first-order, business-oriented session with senior business executives on asset, threat, business consequence, and goals, from the second-order, more technical sessions. (See Figure 3-4).

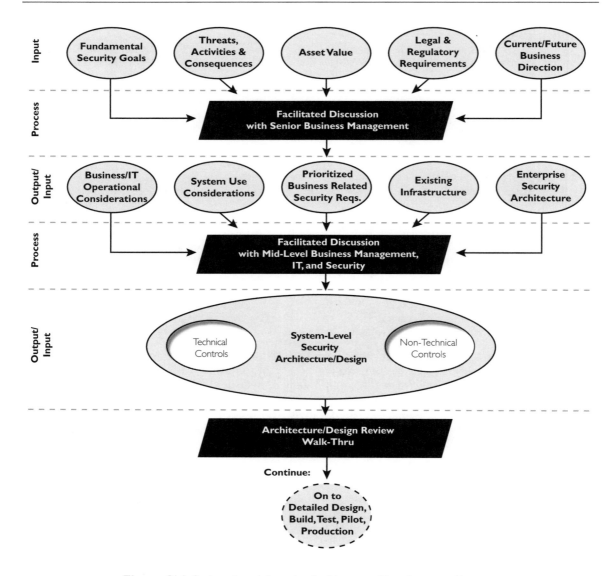

Figure 3-4: System-Level Security Architecture Development Process

The output of the first set of discussions provide the gist for a second series of more technical discussions that cover the second-order architectural/design considerations. These second-order discussions need to include mid-level business management as well as the applications development, IT infrastructure, and security teams.

The second-order considerations include:

- **Business and IT Operational Considerations** – Characterization of business operational and IT operational items that may impact the security sub-architecture. Middle-level managers would examine such concerns. For example:
  - How will new customers be set up and by whom?

- How will users of the system be updated (for example, password resets), or removed from the system?
- Will disparate systems be maintained, or are plans in place to further consolidate the types of systems that are operational within the IT environment?
- Does the organization's security philosophy support central security administration and management, or is a decentralized approach preferred?

- **System Use Considerations** – Who and what will use the system, and when, where, and why will the system be used? For example:
  - Who are the end users of the system (novice or expert user, employee or non-employee, etc.)?
  - From where are users accessing the system (home, office, company network, within the country or across country borders, etc.)?
  - When will users be accessing the system?

- **Current Technical Environment/Architecture** – Characterization and analysis of what may impact the IT infrastructure and either help or impede security.

- **Current Enterprise Security Architecture** – The current and future direction of the organization relative to security. For example, a common goal of enterprise security architecture is to separate the user authentication processing from the applications, thus enabling easier administration of user rights and privileges. Thus, the system architecture team needs to consider if and how this should be accomplished for the system architecture. Further, many organizations are establishing a set of infrastructure security services – PKI or proxies – that the system architecture team may want to, or be forced to, take advantage of.

The system-level security architecture flows out of these second-order discussions, and should include the architecture's specific prioritized goals and requirements. At this level, the output likely includes an initial top-level design, and also non-technical process and procedural controls (often identified in a Concept of Operation (CONOP)).

The final security architecture should attempt to eliminate as many of the security vulnerabilities as possible, and assuage the others as appropriate, given budget considerations relating to the threat and asset value. This is a subtle but very important point.

Some would-be system vulnerabilities can be eliminated altogether by modifying the business or IT processes. If the value of the asset and the extent of the threat warrant, eliminating a vulnerability is often more effective than developing a set of technical or non-technical controls to mitigate it. Other goals that the architecture team should explore include technical or non-technical controls aimed at deterring a would-be attacker, for example, the use of pointed legal language, or advertising the fact that the organization is actively monitoring for malicious activity.

Two final considerations are how to recover from or mitigate the impact of an inadvertent or malicious activity. For example, developing a recovery or failover capability for Denial of Service (DoS) incidents, incorporating the public relations team in the security incident response process to help "media spin" a public embarrassment, or creating backups to assuage the loss or destruction of an asset.

A best practice recommendation at this point in the architecture/design process is to engage the architecture and mid-level business management teams in a bench test – sometimes referred to as a walkthrough. The teams review the theory behind the system-level security architecture and top-level design. They consider the architecture and the non-technical controls under a series of scenarios, and see if the desired goals are achieved prior to moving onto the detailed design (refer to Figure 3-4).

Of course, effective security also requires sound design, construction, testing, implementation, maintenance, and especially training. In addition, since the new system likely runs across existing infrastructure, the architecture team necessarily has to consider whether the current infrastructure provides adequate baseline controls for the new system. In our experience, a significant number of organizations lack appropriate technical security standards and configuration procedures to serve as the basis for a secure infrastructure. Like the proverbial house built on sand, an application hosted on a vulnerable infrastructure is at risk. Thus, you must also include architectural requirements for the associated infrastructure.

Baseline Best Practice Template for Internet Speed

One of the most precious business commodities in the new Internet world is speed. The ability to get to market more quickly with a business system than a competitor – "time to market" – can provide a decided competitive advantage. Thus, the notion that "speed matters" is very appropriate to the new Internet business models. However, the traditional architecture and design process can be a lengthy one, with cycle times that are longer than many Internet business endeavors can endure. Therefore, many best practice organizations adopt new architecture development process models that improve their ability to quickly deploy new architectures in general and security architecture specifically. We recommend the use of best-practice baseline templates. Figure 3-5 shows how an organization can develop and use baseline best-practice architectures to speed up the process.

The premise of this approach is that there is a relatively small number of different types of Web-based systems. Further, similar business systems share a set of similar information protection requirements. These requirements can be enumerated and captured as a predefined set of "best practice" system-level security architecture/design templates. Thus, when business units decide to develop a new business system, the first hurdle for the security team is to decide what type of business system it will be, and to choose the template that it most closely matches. Then the first-order and even the second-order discussions can be focused on where the new business application diverges from the baseline template – this delta is often called the gap in consulting circles. The first facilitated discussions focus on the gap between the typical security goals, threats, assets, vulnerabilities, etc., captured in the template, and the unique requirements of the application at hand. Similarly, the secondary set of discussions would use this gap information as the basis for a rapid development of a new system-level security architecture/design.

In our homebuilding analogy, this process is similar to the use of model homes. Homebuyers can pick a style, customize just a few components, and move into their development tract in short order.

Using baseline best practices also helps you achieve the legal or regulatory standard of due care in protecting company-owned assets, and assets in which the company plays a custodial role. By benchmarking the baseline templates against the industry and continuing to evolve them to meet best practice, the organization takes prudent and responsible steps, which are typically part of the due care considerations that regulators and courts review.

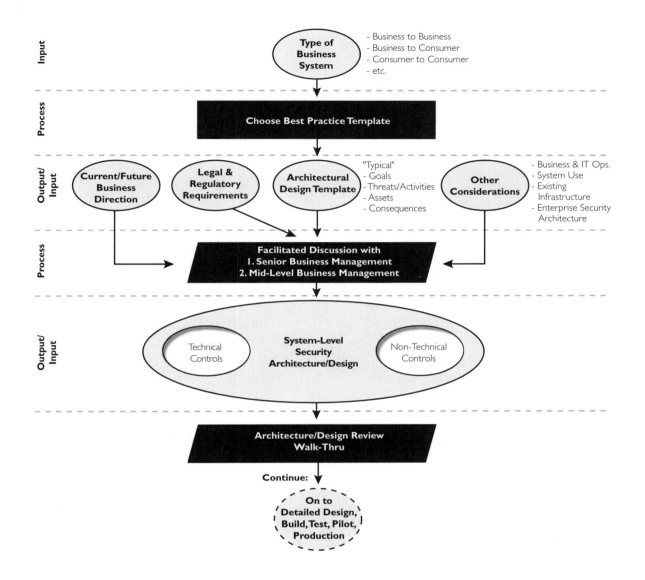

Figure 3-5: Fast-Track System-Level Security Architecture Development Process

Types of Architectures

The number of Web and e-Commerce business applications is growing daily. To implement these, many different common network architectures – such as "business to business" – have emerged over the last few years. In addition to providing a good way to illuminate Web and e-Commerce security architecture/design, the taxonomy of Web applications provides a good first-cut list of baseline templates that organizations should consider developing. Because there are several ways to build a network to support the same e-Commerce and Web-based applications, our taxonomy is based on the business nature of the network rather than its technical implementation.

The taxonomy includes these major Web and e-business applications:

1. **Public Web Presence** – Traditional, organization Web sites for information dissemination. Examples include organizational home pages, news and press releases, product/service descriptions, employment opportunities, and contact information.

2. **Company Intranet Web Site** – Traditional, internal company Web sites supporting information sharing among and across various business functions. Examples include human resources (benefits elections, employee phone book, etc.), finance (financial submission and reporting), engineering and design (project management, distributed design, etc.), and marketing and sales.

3. **Business to Business (B2B)** – Systems that enable enterprises to conduct business with each other by extending the traditional business process and support systems beyond the company borders. Business to Government (B2G) systems share similar characteristics.

4. **Business to Consumer (B2C)** – Applications that enable customers to transact business over the Internet with organizations, and vice-versa.

5. **Consumer to Consumer (C2C)** – Systems providing a cyber place that enables end customers to transact business directly with other customers.

There is no perfect taxonomy of Web/e-Commerce sites, and we realize that a given Web location may be a launch pad for multiple types of applications. This list is illustrative rather than exhaustive.

Figure 3-6 captures the baseline first-order security considerations for the five types of Web and e-business applications. It is important to note that many threats, activities, or consequences could apply to any of the different types of systems. So it is vital for you to relate the key security goals to the most likely risk scenario for a specific system. Otherwise, the architecture team will face such a large number of things to protect against that it will be unable to adequately address critical goals and considerations. As previously mentioned, prioritization is critical for success.

The following sections discuss each of the e-business business applications types, its associated high-level security design template (based on Figure 3-6), and some of the trickier architecture/design considerations.

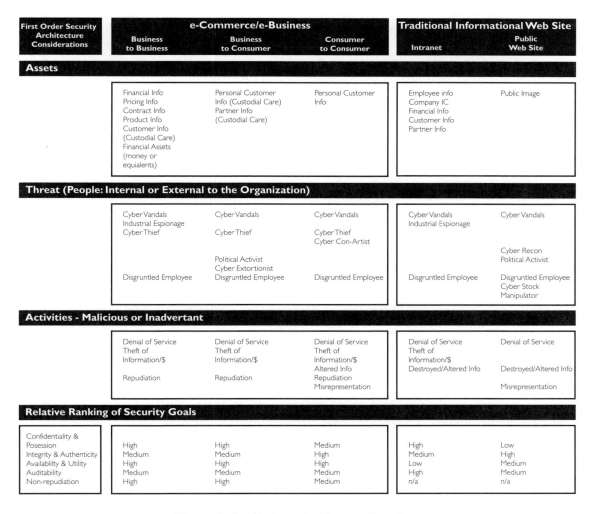

First Order Security Architecture Considerations	e-Commerce/e-Business			Traditional Informational Web Site	
	Business to Business	**Business to Consumer**	**Consumer to Consumer**	**Intranet**	**Public Web Site**
Assets					
	Financial Info Pricing Info Contract Info Product Info Customer Info (Custodial Care) Financial Assets (money or equialents)	Personal Customer Info (Custodial Care) Partner Info (Custodial Care)	Personal Customer Info	Employee info Company IC Financial Info Customer Info Partner Info	Public Image
Threat (People: Internal or External to the Organization)					
	Cyber Vandals Industrial Espionage Cyber Thief	Cyber Vandals Cyber Thief Political Activist Cyber Extortionist	Cyber Vandals Cyber Thief Cyber Con-Artist	Cyber Vandals Industrial Espionage	Cyber Vandals Cyber Recon Political Activist
	Disgruntled Employee	Disgruntled Employee	Disgruntled Employee	Disgruntled Employee	Disgruntled Employee Cyber Stock Manipulator
Activities - Malicious or Inadvertant					
	Denial of Service Theft of Information/$ Repudiation	Denial of Service Theft of Information/$ Repudiation	Denial of Service Theft of Information/$ Altered Info Repudiation Misrepresentation	Denial of Service Theft of Information/$ Destroyed/Altered Info	Denial of Service Destroyed/Altered Info Misrepresentation
Relative Ranking of Security Goals					
Confidentiality & Posession Integrity & Authenticity Availablilty & Utility Auditability Non-repudiation	High Medium High Medium High	High Medium High Medium High	Medium High High Medium Medium	High Medium Low High n/a	Low High Medium Medium n/a

Figure 3-6: e-Business Architecture Templates

Public Web Presence

Public Web sites represent an organization's public image, including product marketing materials, corporate background, and financial information, and other informational content. Public Web sites may contain purely static content, dynamically generated pages, user customization such as My Yahoo!, or data gathering functions such as surveys. Generally speaking, public Web sites are predominantly read-only with little or no need to update information contained in flat files on the local disk or in networked databases. When updates must be performed, they usually relate to storing user-provided information such as personal data to fulfill information requests, survey data, or personalization preferences.

Depending upon the organization sponsoring the public Web site, and its budget and needs, the Web site may be located at the organization's data center, co-located at a service provider, or hosted at a Web hosting provider. Further, the Web site may have to share a server with other applications from the same organization, with other organizations, or perhaps even with other organizations that provide both Web and other application services. Each of these scenarios presents a unique set of security challenges.

High-Level Security Design Template

Figure 3-7 provides an example of a Web site design along with the technical elements to achieve the typical architectural requirements.

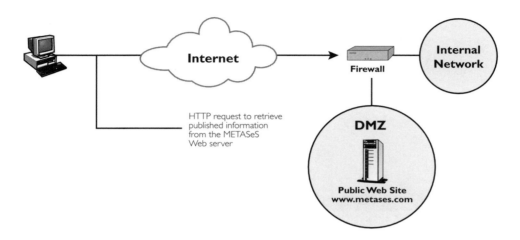

HTTP request to retrieve published information from the METASeS Web server

Figure 3-7: Public Internet Web Site Design

Securing a public Web site can be challenging. By definition, the Web site must be at least partially exposed to the entire world. Accordingly, this means that the server is open to attack from anywhere through any exposed service. One such service is the Hyper Text Transfer Protocol (HTTP), that is, the Web service itself.

Major Security Architecture/Design Challenges

Because the Web server is required to provide access to external users, the threat of attacks in this architecture increase. Attacks may originate from any point on the Internet; sometimes they may be hard to trace and eliminate. The primary security goals are the integrity and availability of the information stored on the Web server.

Integrity addresses the accuracy and completeness of the data. Availability addresses service continuity and support. Bolstering the integrity includes maintaining the security of the system on which the Web server is housed, as well as the Web server's content. In addition, the filtering device must be configured to restrict all types of unauthorized traffic destined for the Web server. Unauthorized traffic includes any protocols or services other than those needed to offer Web server content (for example, HTTP).

Other threats may arise from other applications running on the same physical system as the Web server. For example, an inappropriately configured File Transfer Protocol (FTP) server running on the same physical system could allow arbitrary users to place their own programs on the server. This, perhaps combined with a deficiency in the Web server, could allow a malicious user to execute a program and subsequently gain full control. Once control is taken, the malicious user can alter content on the server, use it to attack other Web sites, or perhaps to attack other systems within an organization.

The situation may become even more grave in a hosted environment where multiple customers maintain their Web presence on one physical server. We have seen cases where compromising a misconfigured public Web site in a hosted environment allows unrestricted access to properly configured extranet Web sites on the same server. Once compromised, access to sensitive corporate data maintained on the extranet Web sites is possible.

The development environments used to create Web sites also pose a security risk. More advanced Web technologies such as Microsoft Active Server Pages (ASPs), Allaire ColdFusion, and Sun Java Server Pages (JSPs), often have subtle, and sometimes not so subtle, security ramifications that are not well understood by many Web site developers. Examples include leaving debugging information on production sites that reveal sensitive information such as database user IDs and passwords, and inadequate access controls that allow arbitrary users to add or modify files. At times, deficiencies in the development languages or related tool sets themselves cause the security vulnerabilities. A recent example is the Microsoft Open Database Connectivity (ODBC) Remote Data Services (RDS) bug, that allows unauthenticated users full access to servers.

Time-to-market pressure upon both development environment vendors and content developers, and resource-constrained system and network administration staff, combined with a lack of security awareness, leave many public Web sites vulnerable to worldwide attack.

Intranet Web Site

This class includes Web-based or Web-enabled sites that provide information to internal employees. They include applications such as a company phone listing, benefits registration system, or a project management system. The major business goal of this class of Web application is information collection and/or dissemination. This category includes static, purely informational sites, sites with more dynamic content, or sites providing a degree of customer interaction (for example a survey, or the ability to change 401K elections).

High-Level Security Design Template

Figure 3-8 illustrates a typical Intranet site design and its technical elements.

Despite the smaller, internal, and, in theory, trusted audience, Intranet site security is still of concern. One survey reported that 71% of respondents detected unauthorized access to sensitive information from corporate insiders.[6]

Major Security Architecture/Design Challenges

The major security goals in the scenario are system security, confidentiality, and content integrity.

In this architecture, a Web server is not exposed to external attacks as in the public Web server architecture. However, it requires equal levels of protection to ward off attacks generated internally by employees or attackers that have accessed the internal network. Internal Web servers are partially protected by a filtering router that controls the traffic traversing the interconnecting subnets.

With regard to development tools and environments, Intranet Web sites share the same security risks and exposures as public Web sites do.

---

[6] 2000 Computer Security Institute/Federal Bureau of Investigation Computer Crime and Security Survey

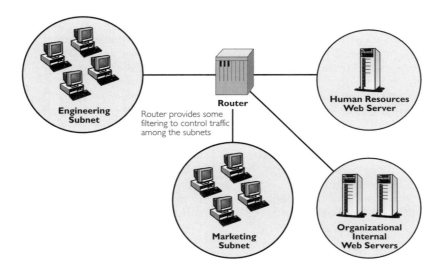

Figure 3-8: Intranet Web Site Design

Business to Business (B2B)

Business to Business (B2B) architectures pertain to informational exchanges between commercial enterprises. This category includes transactions between organizations such as the Automotive Network Exchange (ANX), where multiple automobile manufacturers and vendors can interact to trade goods and information. The ANX network must achieve all the security goals, and meet service requirements such as information exchange, order placement, and subscriber volume.

High-Level Security Design Template

Figure 3-9 provides an example of a business to business architecture in the form of the ANX.

Major Security Architecture/Design Challenges

The major challenges in this architecture are interoperability and standardization of the security solutions. IPSec is the network protocol used to assure confidentiality and authentication. Therefore, interoperability and standardization between diverse implementations of IPSec and encryption key management such as secret key exchange is essential. In addition, availability is an issue that the interacting organizations, for example, the trading partners, require in order to maintain business continuity. If a critical network element, such as a router or an encryption device, fails, it restricts the affected organization from communicating with other organizations.

In Figure 3-9, the major network elements that help achieve this architecture include the IPSec-compliant devices (for example, routers or firewalls), CCAs (Certified Certificate Authorities) for key management, and CISPs (Certified Internet Service Providers) for connectivity.

Given the high dollar value of transactions that usually occur in business-to-business relationships, there is considerable interest in using strong authentication measures such as Public Key Infrastructure (PKI) and the digital certificate authorities. However, deploying a PKI is

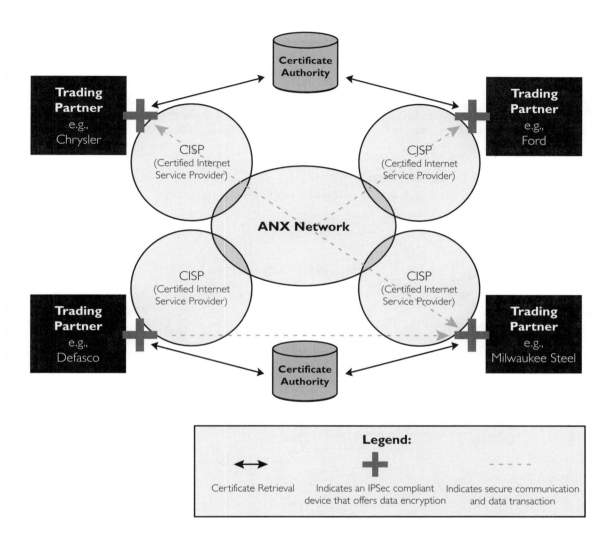

Figure 3-9: Business to Business Network Architecture -- ANX (Automotive Network Exchange) Example

not a panacea despite its potential benefits. There are many significant political, policy, functional, and technical issues. These include the fundamental concerns of who do you trust and how much do you trust them, the technical interoperability of the multi-vendor architecture, and who is liable in case the infrastructure is compromised or fraudulent transactions are conducted.

Business to Consumer (B2C)

A business to consumer (B2C) architecture pertains to transactions between organizations and clients and customers. It includes financial services such as on-line trading and banking, on-line shopping, and even tax-return submission. Confidentiality is one of the main requirements from the perspective of customers, who demand that the submitted information is handled with the highest security. The organization must assure that the customer information remains confidential not only during transit but after submission. Typically, communication between customers and an organization's Web site can be encrypted through strong encryption techniques, for example, 128-bit SSL (Secure Socket Layer). With such methods, the data in transit is difficult to decipher and obtain in clear text, and attacks through network monitoring or sniffing are not feasible.

Attackers typically target the Web server, the end host where the information is kept. Therefore, the organization should ensure the highest security measures to protect the Web server from attacks based on the objectives defined in the Information Security Goals section.

High-Level Security Design Template

Figure 3-10 provides an example of a business to consumer architecture.

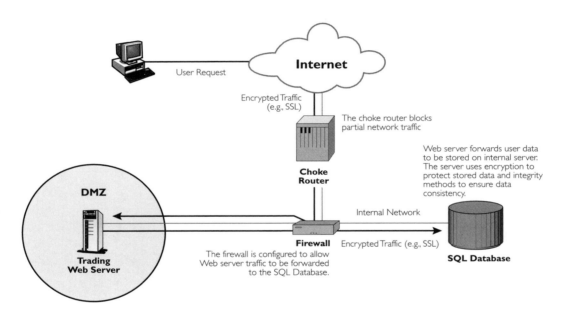

Figure 3-10: Business to Consumer Network Architecture

In such a system, the end user expects that submitted information is handled with the highest security. Confidentiality is one of the main goals. On-line stock brokerage firms are typical applications. The organization offering the service should ensure the user information remains confidential, not only during transit but also after submission. Typically, the communication between an end user and an organization's Web site can be encrypted using strong encryption (for example, 128-bit SSL). Thus, the data in transit is hard to decipher, and attacks such as network monitoring are not feasible.

Attackers typically target the end host, where the information is kept in the Web server. Therefore, the organization should stress the building of security measures to protect it. These measures are based on the security goals defined in the section Information Security Goals (see Figure 3-1).

Major Security Architecture/Design Challenges

All the same issues that apply to public Web sites also apply to business to consumer sites. The entire world is again a potential customer, so restricting access to a subset of the population is impossible. The security risk, however, of operating a business to consumer site is greater than in the case of a public Web site, as there is more than corporate reputation on the line. Consumer privacy and access to financial information can also be targets.

Most of the responsibility for security requirements falls on the organization offering a service. The two major areas of information protection are transmission and storage. During the transmission of the data – between the consumer and the organization's Web server, or between the Web server and the organization's internal database systems – confidentiality and integrity must be maintained. Regarding storage, you must maintain availability (for example, backup and recovery) and confidentiality (for example, data integrity inspection, stored data encryption, and authenticated retrieval requests).

The major underlying network elements include the user software and its ability to comply with encryption requirements (for example, SSL with 128-bit key encryption); the Web server that collects user information and queries back-end systems; database systems that maintain related data; and intermediate filtering devices such as routers or firewalls, proxy, reverse proxy, etc., that provide additional encryption or filtering.

Because of the nature of the transactions conducted at business to consumer Web sites, there needs to be a high degree of integration between the Web servers, local back-end databases, and often the fulfillment systems, clearinghouses, or suppliers that the Web sites do not own or operate. This interconnection of systems crosses corporate boundaries and transforms itself into a business to business operation, sharing the same risks associated with a pure business to business site.

Consumer to Consumer (C2C)

Consumer to consumer (C2C) architectures apply to such online applications as Web-based auction sites where consumers can exchange goods such as cars, antiques, and used computers.

High-Level Security Design Template

Figure 3-11 provides an example of a consumer to consumer network in the guise of an online auction business.

Under such a scenario, the on-line auction provider sets the security goals. The provider ensures that transactions such as bids, postings, or shipment of goods are secure and reliable.

Major Security Architecture/Design Challenges

The major design challenges require that this architecture ensure authentication, non-repudiation, data integrity, and confidentiality and availability. Participating parties must provide certain information to verify their identities before transactions are honored, thus achieving authentication and non-repudiation. To protect the transacted data that is transmitted across the network or stored on the transaction site's Web server, encryption methods such as SSL is used for user-to-server and server-to-server connections. 3DES, BlowFish, or other encryption is used for local data storage. A filtering device such as a firewall or router can control traffic between the protected network, where sensitive information customarily resides, and the Internet or other trustless networks.

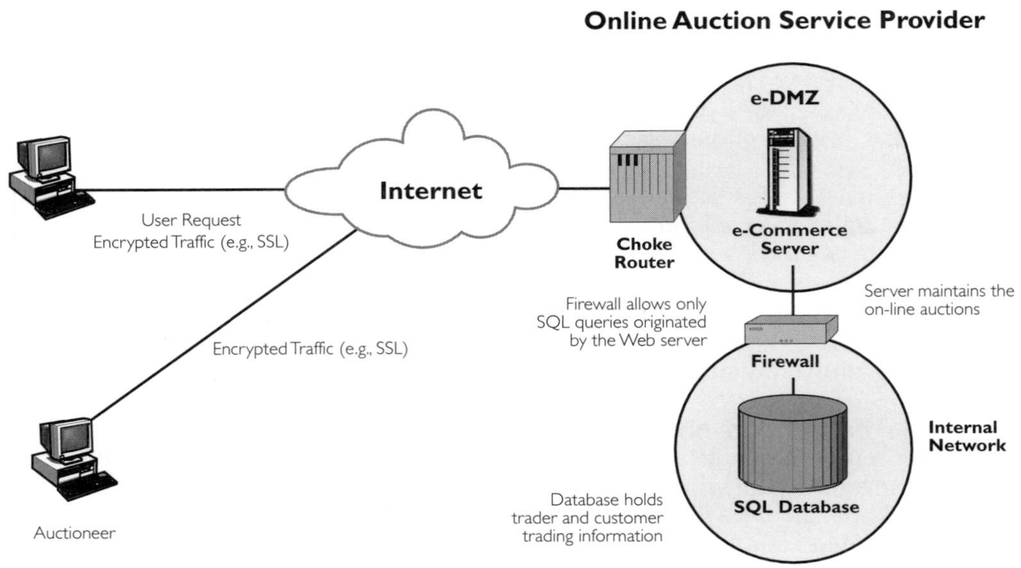

Figure 3-11: Consumer to Consumer Network Architecture

Summary

Despite the diversity of scenarios presented, ranging from simple informational Web sites to complex B2B offerings, each scenario is built on the same fundamental infrastructure. The challenges and templates presented above are by no means a comprehensive reference for all Web sites. Your organization needs to perform its own due diligence for determining acceptable safeguards, drawing on the above outline of different architectures as a building block.

System Development Life Cycle (SDLC) Methodology

With the increasing use of Internet applications and e-Commerce, system and business functions are no longer isolated. To produce a secure application, careful planning and design across groups are essential. Performance requirements and hardware environments must be explicitly defined at the start of a project to leverage optimal security measures. Communication between different functional units is imperative. On-going participation of developers, operations, security staff, and clients increases the chances of a project that is on time and cost-effective and that satisfies customer requirements.

Among the major reasons projects fail are lack of user input, incomplete requirements, and the inability to manage changing requirements. Other reasons are inconsistent application development and slack access controls, as well as rushed time-to-market deployment. Concerning this last point, compressed schedules likely truncate the design phase and reduce valuable information exchanges between developers and other project teams, leading to less than fully secure software. Other reasons for project failure are limited use of testing or quality assurance. The tangible and intangible costs of code that contains errors, even if it is part of a product that is first to market, may outweigh the initial revenue generated.

You need a set of methodologies to produce and deliver successful software and to ensure the process is manageable, complies with standards, and keeps budget costs under control. The most systematic way to avoid costly mistakes is for the program manager to firmly apply the "three team, three process" combination of:

- System Development Life Cycle (SDLC)
- Software Quality Assurance
- Software Change Control

These methodologies are usually implemented through separate teams. The design and development team addresses the more technical aspects of development in the software life cycle (Figure 3-12). The Quality Assurance (QA) team implements the software quality assurance plan to test the software and maintain program value. The operations team implements new versions of the product through software change control. These three methodologies are discussed in the sections that follow.

System Development Life Cycle (SDLC)

Securing the underlying infrastructure of an e-Commerce system provides only partial protection against intrusions. Application security needs to be accorded the same, if not greater, importance, as the application is the interface between the organization and the end user.

System resources can be rendered vulnerable where security defects or flaws in interoperability enter the production environment without the knowledge of developers. Two kinds of "failure cost" may result. Internal failure costs entail repair of programs and re-engineering, as well as loss of critical data, customer lists, and trade secrets or other proprietary information. External failure costs entail both tangible costs, such as technical support, warranty expenses, or lost revenue, and intangible costs, such as loss of brand equity or customer goodwill. Software development that incorporates security concepts and practices from the start is likely more effective as well as less expensive, as such an approach reduces both kinds of cost.

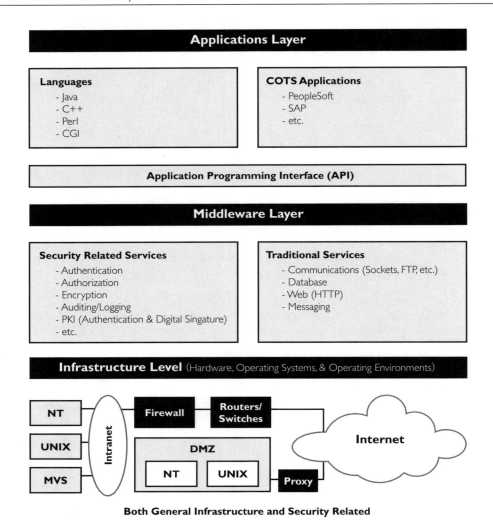

Figure 3-12: System Development Life Cycle (SDLC) -- Systems, Applications, & Infrastructure

To successfully deploy secure Web and e-Commerce applications, security should be incorporated during all life cycle phases, from requirements, to architecture and design, development, testing, deployment/implementation, and operations/maintenance (see Figure 3-13).

While Figure 3-13 is akin to an iterative, "waterfall" development process, other approaches, such as Rapid Application Development (RAD), similarly need to incorporate security.

Security Concerns and the System Development Life Cycle (SDLC)

In today's Internet environment, software systems are much more vulnerable to security risks. Yet the security aspects of computer applications development are too often ignored, given low priority, mishandled, or simply misunderstood. Many application development and business teams do not understand or know how to handle the new risks. Quite a few

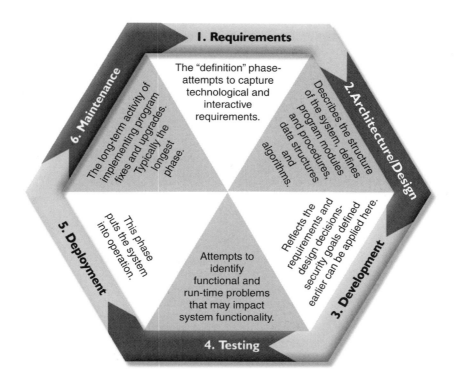

Figure 3-13: The System Development Life Cycle (SDLC)

development teams and business teams – in human resources, manufacturing, finance, etc. – are not properly trained in the security aspects of application development. Some are aware in a general way or at a high level of increased security risks, but not at the detailed or application levels that involve knowledge of security procedures and techniques.

Further, many organizations often treat security as an afterthought. This attitude leads to either insecure applications, or to considerable expense when security fixes have to be retrofitted.

Security teams have to work more closely with the application, infrastructure, and business teams to train them on defending against the potential weaknesses in information systems and procedures that intruders and threats can exploit.

An initial step is to make the application teams aware that security is an issue. They must learn to make this an overt design point in new systems. A follow-on step that many organizations should take is to provide security assistance, such as training, architecture assistance, and review teams.

At the same time, it is important for application developers to realize that not every risk should be handled the same way. Not everything in your organization can be or should be completely protected against attack. You want to fashion an "appropriate" level of security controls based on the value of an asset and the risk posed to it.

Further, security needs to incorporate both technical and non-technical controls. More importantly, it must be integrated into the applications and infrastructure instead of bolted on afterwards. It should be addressed in each phase of the life cycle, from requirements and design to maintenance and operations. If you do not address a concern in its respective phase, it will only pose more of a risk and be more expensive and more difficult to fix later on.

The METASeS report, *Secure System Development Life Cycle (SDLC)*, discusses the security aspects of software development in depth. For detailed information on application security, see the METASeS report, *Building Secure e-Commerce Applications*.

System Development Life Cycle (SDLC) Phases

This section discusses the steps in the system development life cycle (SDLC). By "system" we mean a Web or e-Commerce application and its underlying infrastructure. The SDLC phases vary from organization to organization. The standard phases that we discuss are:

1. Requirements
2. Architecture and Design
3. Development
4. Testing
5. Deployment/Implementation
6. Maintenance/Operations

All of these phases are addressed below. Note that the discussion of tasks for each phase is representative, not all-inclusive. Our aim is to highlight the most important tasks for your consideration.

Requirements

The requirements or requirements definition phase of the application life cycle attempts to capture most of the necessary technological and interactive requirements of the system. E-Commerce applications should incorporate security requirements, as well ensure that the system can address current security needs and provide scalability for future security needs.

This phase defines the software project, and outlines the parameters required for its accomplishment. The requirements document should include a description of customer requirements, a definition of the product, and the functions or operations the program must perform and support. Other requirements may be included for performance criteria (memory limits, time benchmarking, user accessibility, etc.) or platform requirements (hardware environment, devices, compatibility, etc.) The requirements document must include measures to ensure program security.

Among the issues you might address in the requirements phase of an e-Commerce application are:

- Analyze security requirements and goals.

- Identify the user communities that employ the application, for example, administrators, employees, customers, business partners, etc.

- Perform risk analysis and asset value analysis.

- Review regulatory requirements.

- Understand customer partner interface requirements.

- Identify profiles for each user community.

- Formulate priorities and budget constraints.

Architecture and Design

The architecture and design describe the structure of the system. They define the program modules and procedures, and the data structures and algorithms. Plans for producing documentation and test cases may be produced at this stage. Architecture and design translates and maps the requirements to the appropriate system components and details how they interface with each other. Software modifications required for different platforms are also handled in this phase.

Top-level security considerations to incorporate during the architecture and design phase include:

- Develop infrastructure security architecture.

- Develop high-level application security architecture that is linked with infrastructure architecture, as well as authentication, authorization, secure transactions, user side security (for example, certificates), and secure software/component distribution.

- Perform architecture walkthrough.

Examples of detailed security considerations to incorporate are:

- Define the major system components, and note if their interaction requires authentication and encryption. Establish a list of acceptable authentication and encryption mechanisms, and indicate whether third-party products are required (for example, SecurID, S/Key). (S/Key is a mechanism for authenticating to a system with a user ID used in conjunction with a one-time password.)

- Define external systems with which the e-Commerce system interfaces, such as certificate authorities, database servers, or mail servers.

- For each external system that must interface directly with the e-Commerce applications, define the communication protocols (for example, TCP/IP) and the interaction mechanisms (for example, RPC, SQL, or Common Gateway Interface (CGI)) to establish encryption and authentication methods.

- Define the user interfaces and how they interact with the system (for example, Web browsers, Java applets, or JavaScript), and incorporate them with the user profile and authentication requirements.

- For each interface, define the user data required to be captured (for example, user IDs, passwords, credit card numbers, Social Security numbers, etc.) Assign each a sensitivity value (for example, public=0, secret=3). Also for each interface, identify its underlying communication channel and incorporate encryption requirements.

- Identify authentication mechanisms, such as permissions, that each identified user community should employ to interface with the system. Be sure to analyze rights and permissions for each user profile.

- Identify, segment, and prioritize the data that the system handles.

- Identify mechanisms such as encryption that protect critical data.

- Identify the data required to be transmitted over an unprotected network. If the data contains sensitive information, establish requirements to provide the means, such as encryption (for example, SSL), for its appropriate protection.

- Identify external systems with which the application interfaces, such as SQL databases or legacy systems, and assess security capabilities that these systems can offer or use in order to protect data transmission and management. Identify functional requirements for interfacing with external systems. Such interfaces might include CGI scripts, FTP transfers, or SQL queries.

- Assess known application and infrastructure vulnerabilities.

- Include security requirements in system and network performance and hardware sizing.

- Ensure selected hardware performs when additional security services are running.

- Develop detailed application security design.

- Develop detailed infrastructure security design.

- Develop security configuration standards.

- Develop an integration plan.

- Perform design review. This should include technical reviews geared to both the application level and the infrastructure level.

- Design a security test plan, including a plan for testing compliance.

- Develop policies and document them for the various parties involved (development, integration, customers, partners, etc.)

- Develop technical standards.

- Decide on the insourcing or outsourcing of a security solution.

Development

The development phase reflects the requirements and design decisions. The security goals defined earlier can be applied during this phase. For example, the proper policies and procedures should be in place to protect the integrity and confidentiality of the code, designs, and the underlying development infrastructure from attacks such as theft or destruction.

A key part of development is coding, that is, the writing of the actual programming code. Some companies have coding standards – specific rules for code structure, appearance, and security. Standards can prolong the life of the code, and make it easier to maintain. Writing correct, secure code from the start saves time and money during testing, assists the organization in being first to market, and reduces costs in production execution, thereby maintaining customer satisfaction and resource security.

You should maintain three separate environments for development, testing, and production. The development area deals with coding and application development. The testing area supports acceptance testing of code. (Changes to the software are not permitted in the testing environment. Instead, they are performed in development and then tested again.) The production area supports access to production data, that is, code that is ready for public use. You should put system source code and related configuration files in a secure environment, one that is isolated from the rest of the network.

Note that the METASeS report, *Building Secure e-Commerce Applications*, discusses in detail the security issues relating to application development.

To ensure that the code is secure, developers should use defensive programming techniques (Figure 3-14).

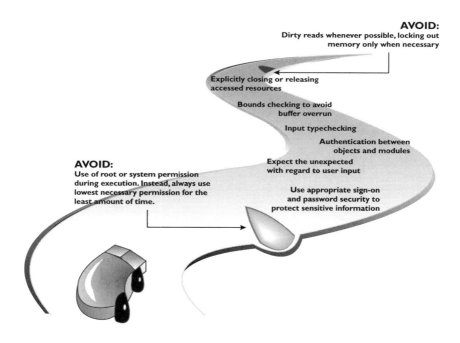

Figure 3-14: Defensive Programming -- The Road to Security

Examples of development phase security considerations are:

- Identify, in terms of security, the weaknesses and strengths of the programming language used to develop each component.

- Place user input inspection mechanisms in each defined user interface to ensure that improper data does not traverse it or is stored in the system through it. Improper or malicious user input is one of the leading causes of fraud or system compromises. If the system does not check the user input, then the fundamental principle of data I/O will result: "garbage in and garbage out." In case of an e-Commerce application, that bromide may be amended, in a positive light, to "carefully crafted input and sensitive information output."

- Put system source code and related configuration files in a secure environment, preferably one isolated from the rest of the network.

- For data transmission across untrusted networks, deploy appropriate encryption authentication mechanisms.

- Train developers on using security-related middleware and secure coding practices.

- Train infrastructure teams on installation and configuration of the middleware.

- Establish inspection modules and mechanisms to inspect the integrity of the data exchanged between the e-Commerce application and the interfacing system.

- Ensure that logging of user and component interaction is incorporated in the system.

- Set up a code/component version control system. Ensure control and integrity of the source code and component configurations.

- Code application-level security components.

- Purchase, install, and configure security tools in a test lab. (There are suites of tools that detect buffer overflows, ensure use of all declared variables, etc.)

- Develop operational procedures. Ensure that network and systems administrators, partners, customers, and integration firms that deploy the solution or solution components meet the requirements outlined in the technical standards for the mitigation of vulnerabilities.

- Develop configuration guides that outline implementation procedures.

- Update the disaster recovery/business resumption plan.

- Set up security-related "bug" or vulnerability tracking. Ensure that identified vulnerabilities are systematically tracked.

Testing

The testing phase attempts to identify functional and run-time problems that may impact system functionality. As such, you should develop strong testing methodology to ensure the detection of most errors before deployment.

Systematic and thorough testing minimizes system vulnerabilities. A complete testing strategy verifies the system is secure and keeps vulnerabilities to a minimum.

Testing determines if the system is effective, that is, whether it is correct, reliable, efficient, usable, maintainable, and portable. An organized testing strategy generates confidence in the product by identifying bugs, application deficiencies, and security problems. The testing phase uses several levels of resolution: through individual modules, full-scale integration, functionality, accuracy, and regression testing. The test plan may be started in the design phase to capture specific test objectives for single modules as well as for the larger, integrated program.

In addition to the typical testing methodology, among the actions you might take to inspect security on e-Commerce applications are:

- Conduct a code review or code walkthrough. Verify that application code meets security requirements and specifications.

- Perform run-time profiling for execution trees, loops, memory usage, etc.

- Test configuration procedures. Verify that administrators can use the procedures to set up network and systems components to meet the standards.

- Perform a systems test. Verify technical components are functioning according to design and architecture specifications.

- Conduct a performance/load test.

- Perform usability testing of applications with security controls. Verify that applications with security controls meet customer usability/ergonomic needs, and make suitable adjustments.

- Establish a penetration testing methodology that aims to exploit application vulnerabilities such as buffer overflows, buffer underflows, cookie manipulation, user authentication, user tracking, and session hijacking.

- Perform attacks that aim to render the application system useless for authorized and unauthorized users. This provides an analysis of the impact that a similar attack has on the system, and permits development of appropriate mitigation.

- Perform vulnerability assessments against the underlying infrastructure.

- Perform, or at least assess, Denial of Service (DoS) attacks against the underlying infrastructure to identify weaknesses that may impact the network and application, and supply mechanisms for mitigation.

- Perform drills to ensure that the disaster recovery procedures can be executed in a timely manner without disruptions or lack of resources. Make sure that new applications are added to the disaster recovery or business resumption plan.

- Conduct system testing in a secure environment, preferably one on an isolated network segment.

- Incorporate testing from a third party to provide non-biased assessment.

Deployment/Implementation

The deployment/implementation phase puts the system into operation.

During this phase, among the steps you might take are:

- Deploy a full-pilot solution that encompasses infrastructure and applications. Ensure that the deployment processes work, that the applications work in a live business trial, and that the operational processes, including security operations, are in order.

- Enable the various teams to tune the application and infrastructure, and make deployment and operational process adjustments prior to a full-scale implementation.

- Conduct the transition between the final system test and the deployment environment through secure means such as encrypted transmissions over a secure network or protected media (for example, CD-ROM with encrypted contents). This should minimize threats associated with data interception. Otherwise, an attacker might obtain a copy of all the system components that help him perform analysis to either reverse-engineer the system or pinpoint security weaknesses.

- Ensure that the system's files are authentic (for example, using digital signatures or making comparisons to the originals).

- Perform regression testing to ensure that system components provide complete functionality as designed.

- Implement security policies and procedures with the deployment to assist in management and administrative tasks.

- Familiarize administrative personnel with the security functions of the system.

- Perform additional vulnerability assessment, using all plausible user scenarios – Internet user, customer, business partner etc. – to ensure that the environment has not introduced system vulnerabilities.

- Execute the code conversion.

- Deploy a training and awareness program. Train administrative personnel and users in the system's security functions.

- Deploy the full-scale solution.

Maintenance/Operations

Maintenance/operations is the long-term activity of implementing program fixes and upgrades. It is typically the longest phase for any software system, and incorporates administrative tasks required to keep the system in optimal operation.

In addition to typical system maintenance requirements, the following are among the security-related tasks you might take:

- Monitor the health of the underlying systems and applications.

- Ensure that policies and procedures are enforced through scheduled reviews.

- Perform scheduled system security checks to verify account activity, system integrity, permissions, and resource access.

- Test and migrate ("promote") software updates.

- Perform scheduled disaster recovery drills to ensure that resources are available and procedures are carried out without interruption.

- Perform scheduled system backups, data encryption, and data storage in a secure location.

- Establish a test system to test new releases and patches before deployment.

- Keep the policy and procedure documents up to date.

- Perform scheduled network penetration tests to ensure that new vulnerabilities are discovered and addressed in a timely manner.

- Conduct periodic vulnerability assessments.

- Perform auditing, logging, monitoring, and archiving.

Software Quality Assurance

Software Quality Assurance (SQA) is a program of action for prevention, early detection, and efficient removal or modification of defects from software products. An SQA plan assigns quality assurance roles and responsibilities, and includes SQA activities in the project schedule.

SQA elements include:

- **Quality Management Approach** – Organizational approach to customer satisfaction involving customers, staff, suppliers and processes. The basic principles of total quality management are: 1) the involvement and respect of everyone associated with the organization; 2) continual improvement of the processes used to prepare and deliver products and services to the customer; and 3) preventing problems, not waiting for them to occur.

- **Effective Software Engineering Technology** – As part of the project design, the technology used to design and support a software product, that is, development tools, applications and platforms. It must be sufficient to perform the desired tasks and maintain the project for the projected life of the program. Consideration must be taken for internal and external compatibilities, performance parameters, and durability.

- **Formal Technical Review** – Provides feedback to management on the status of the product. It normally takes place at the conclusion of a development phase. Upon a successful review, the decision is made to proceed to the next phase of development. Technical reviews may include:

  - System requirements review
  - Test readiness review
  - System design review
  - Software specification review
  - Preliminary design review
  - Critical design review

- Functional configuration audit
- Physical configuration audit

- **Multi-Tiered Testing Strategy** – Includes separate tests for component, functional unit, integration and system testing. The test documentation includes the test plans, test design/cases, test procedures, and test report. This documentation defines the test objectives, requirements, staff/resources, facilities/equipment, expected/actual results, data evaluation, and recommendations.

- **Control of Software and Documentation** – Required to track the changes made to the software: a description of the change, the rationale for the change, and the identification of affected baselines. The absence of software control management documentation can become significant when a reviewer at final product evaluation tries to identify whether the software products under evaluation are actually those products that were verified and validated.

- **Compliance Procedures** – Enables the appropriate monitoring of the software and the development process that produces it for compliance with established standards and procedures. Ensures that any inadequacies in the product, process, or standards are brought to management's attention.

- **Measurement of Reporting Mechanisms** – Communicates information on specific deficiencies in the software, or summarizes specific tasks or groups of tasks performed during the development, testing, auditing, and monitoring phases. Measurement criteria based on metrics data or statistical control limits determines actions required to repair the software. Reports should be generated as necessary (for example, for each anomaly or at the completion of each major task), and used during formal reviews that assess the current product and development activities, as well as to improve the development process for future projects.

SQA applies consistent quality throughout the Software Life Cycle. In effect, it functions as an oversight body. Personnel other than developers should perform the QA duties. After all, developers are often too wrapped up with the code to evaluate it impartially. You should have an impartial third party sign off on the code.

Software Change Control

Software change control is the process of managing and controlling changes that are requested after the approval of the system requirements document. It is a structured maintenance mechanism that tracks software modifications and controls version releases to enable a systematic, managed distribution. Sound software security management requires procedures to manage application change control and clearly define systems changes. Updates performed within a well-defined change control process are less likely to expose system code or resources to risk. The typical steps for a change control procedure are:

1. Evaluate and develop the required change.

2. Complete a change request form.

3. Analyze the impact of the requested change.

4. Take initial action on the request.

5. Determine the effect of the requested change.

It is essential that required software changes are authorized and approved, thoroughly tested, sufficiently documented, and implemented at an appropriate time. Documentation for each software change should be completed and accepted before changes are made to production. Migrating the changes to production is another area that requires a separation of responsibilities to avoid a "quick fix," which may generate more problems than it solves. An operations team dedicated to version control and procedure compliance should transfer the software from the test to the production environment. Software change control helps prevent people from slipping alterations into production code, be they benign but wrong-headed changes or malicious, backdoor exploits. It also lets you roll back to a previous version of the system if the changes have a negative impact on the system.

Recommendations for Software Development Methodology

Our general suggestions for software life cycle, QA, and change control follow:

- For software developers and security personnel, put policies, standards and procedures in place as the guidelines for compliance and accountability.

- For contractors working on software development and security, ensure that policies, standards and procedures define the contractual requirements for compliance and accountability. Furthermore, put strict limitations in place for contractor access to company data.

- Make sure that three separate teams or functional units exist for software life cycle, quality assurance, and change control.

- Train developers in defensive programming techniques such as performing authentication between objects, modules, and devices, closing opened resources, handling the pitfalls of buffer overruns, releasing temporary memory, etc. Make the QA team familiar with these techniques.

- Employ access control techniques with application components. Allow only authorized users access to production changes.

- Develop program requirements that are complete and mutually agreed upon by the relevant groups.

- Undertake migration of software between environments only after obtaining the appropriate sign-offs specified in the software change control procedures.

- Require that a software change request treats multiple modules as a single unit. This ensures that individual modules cannot be put into production until all related modules are functioning properly.

- Put in place a contingency plan to restore the software to its previous version.

- Ensure that purchased software (commercially off the shelf (COTS) or by contract), as opposed to internally developed software, also meets security specifications. Enforce policies and procedures to integrate external products, including change control and SQA testing of security functions.

The Underlying Infrastructure Components

Each of the underlying architectural components plays a part in the security puzzle. Some of the items are specifically designed as security controls, some have inherent security capabilities, and still others are inherently insecure. You need to have some level of understanding of each of the elements, and what positive or negative role each one plays in e-Commerce security.

During the design of an e-Commerce application, you should identify the underlying infrastructure that houses the system. The e-Commerce system is not only dependent on the server deployed, but also on the neighboring network components and other systems with which it interfaces.

The location of components can be particularly important when assessing the overall risk of your e-Commerce application. For example, locating your server on a very congested network segment or behind an overworked firewall may negatively impact your overall application. Likewise, from a traditional security standpoint, placing your authentication server on an unprotected, insecure network may open your application up to unnecessary security compromise.

We divide the infrastructure components into these broad categories:

1. Network Infrastructure and Services, such as routers and Web servers
2. Security Infrastructure and Services, such as firewalls and VPNs

Network Infrastructure and Services

The following elements, discussed below, are incorporated in a typical e-Commerce system:

- Routers
- Domain Name System (DNS) servers
- Mail servers
- Web servers
- Remote access servers
- Authentication server
- X.500 or Lightweight Directory Access Protocol (LDAP)-based Directory services
- Servers/Operating Systems (OS)
- Desktops/Operating Systems (OS)

Each element is discussed below.

Routers

Routers are basic network devices used to interconnect networks – IP networks in the context of this document. They are workhorses that forward traffic across the Internet, and throughout internal networks.

Some of the primary features of routers include the ability to simultaneously control several different protocols such as TCP/IP, IPX (Internetwork Packet eXchange), SNA (Systems Network Architecture) or physical delivery platform such as Frame Relay. Routers also provide QoS (Quality of Service) to improve performance and utilization or provide the means for network segmentation.

Figure 3-15 provides a typical network topology emphasizing routers along with common network protocols.

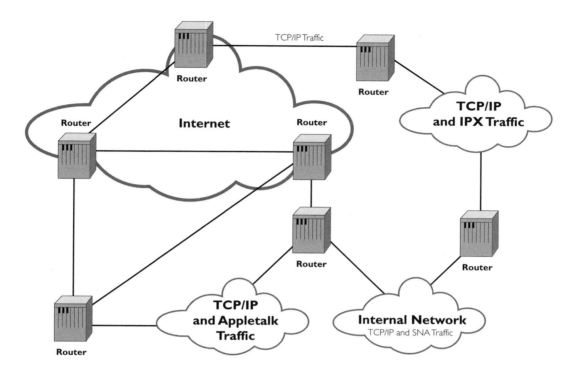

Figure 3-15: Routers Topology

As shown in the figure, routers can handle internal organizational network traffic, or "public" network traffic that traverses through external networks such as the Internet.

Unlike any other network or desktop-based elements discussed in this section, you cannot connect to the Internet without a router. If you have a small, low-traffic connection to the Internet, the router may reside with your ISP, which is responsible for maintaining and configuring it. If yours is a high-traffic, multi-component Internet gateway, you may have multiple routers deployed in your gateway network, extranet, or boundary subnet, in addition to dozens or hundreds of routers on your internal network. In addition to their main task of sending network packets to the correct destination, routers can perform several security functions. These include packet screening or filtering, traffic logging, and segregation of network traffic among subnets. Routers can be used very effectively to enforce policy, for example, by disallowing certain types of traffic in or out of a network, filtering traffic from or to particular destinations, or logging the volume, time, or source and destination of selected types of traffic.

However, their critical role, broad capability, and complete exposure also make routers a very attractive target for attackers. Routers that have not been properly configured or maintained can be subverted or compromised such that they allow undesirable traffic, monitor the contents of network traffic, or broadcast false information to other network devices.

It is very important, therefore, to establish documented, uniform, and *secure* practices for configuring and maintaining routers on your organization's network, and in particular, at the borders where your network joins to other networks. Some of the actions you might consider taking are:

- Alter the configuration of the network element by removing default settings such as default user accounts and network protocols and services. This limits the number of potential vulnerabilities an intruder may take advantage of to attack the system. One of the first methods that attackers use to gain access to a system is try to exploit default configuration settings such as user IDs and passwords. When installing new routers, change all factory default settings for passwords and SNMP (Simple Network Management Protocol) community strings.

- Test router configuration rule sets and Access Control Lists (ACLs) in a controlled environment using a network monitor to ensure that guidelines are carried out as intended. For example, you want to confirm that traffic you intended to block is, in fact, being blocked. (Rule sets, also known as access control lists, are the instructions that tell the router how to behave.)

- Place router configuration rule sets under configuration management, so that changes may be controlled and tracked, and rolled back, if necessary.

- You should establish exception handling procedures for requests to allow otherwise restricted traffic through a router. Personnel who maintain routers need policy guidance to assist in making decisions about what should be allowed or disallowed.

- There is often a need to manage routers remotely, either by dialing into the router over a phone line, or by connecting to the router over the network, perhaps using a designated management port. For high-risk, high-exposure border routers, best practices suggest the use of strong one-time passwords or hardware authentication tokens, as reusable passwords can be cracked or sniffed over the network. Lower-risk internal routers may not require measures as strong.

- Many organizations manage their routers with specialized software packages. Before installing a package, check for security advisories relevant to the software. Be sure that the package itself can be installed and used securely, including support for strong authentication, and secure (encrypted) channels from the end devices to the central console.

Note that routers positioned in an internal network provide, by segmenting the internal network, some level of protection against attacks. For example, a router can segment business divisions such as human resources, legal, marketing, or engineering into their respective networks, thus limiting access from one network to another based on the origin of the traffic.

Domain Name System (DNS) Servers

The Domain Name System (DNS) in the Internet maps host names, to IP addresses or other resource record values. The name space of the Internet is divided into domains, where the responsibility for managing names within each domain is delegated hierarchically to designated primary and secondary servers. These machines are referred to as "name servers" or "DNS servers." There must be at least two DNS servers per registered domain. However, many different domains may use the same DNS servers as their respective name servers. This allows for failover if the primary system happens to be offline, or is disconnected from the section of the network on which the secondary name server resides.

There are two types of domain name numbering: 1) registered Internet Protocol (IP) numbers; and 2) RFC 1918 numbers. RFC 1918 is entitled Address Allocation for Private Internets, the so-called "10 dot" numbers for internal-only device identification. These numbers never go out onto the Internet, a fact that which frees up "real" IP addresses in what is a very tight address space.

When a commercial entity decides to register a domain name, it currently has to select from a few Top Level Domains (TLDs). An example of a TLD is .com. An organization's .com name and other names fall under that designation. They make up an accurate naming structure for the organization's network-addressable information systems.

The proper configuration and placement of DNS servers is critical for security. Many protocols treat the domain name received from a DNS query as authoritative information. It is common to find many authentication programs that base the trust given on the domain name alone. This poses a problem if someone is able to compromise your DNS server and change records to indicate that their system is to be regarded as trusted.

Given the critical role of the DNS server, you should have a well-defined policy that provides strict guidelines for deploying and maintaining the DNS hierarchy. Some of our recommended guidelines follow:

- Your external DNS server should contain the minimum amount of records necessary for your organization to successfully conduct business on the Internet. It should not advertise internal host names nor have information on hardware or operating systems. Such information is very useful to intruders trying to penetrate your network.

- The internal users of your network require DNS services for their day-to-day activities. Your primary DNS server represents your organization by actually performing the DNS queries and sending the results back to your internal network. The best way to accommodate this with a firewall is to designate one DNS server on the internal network. All hosts internal to the network should point to this one DNS server for resolution. In turn, the firewall policy should state that all outbound queries should be allowed only from the one internal DNS server to one external DNS server.

- The host platform for any DNS server should have the latest version of the operating system, all the patches, and the most recent version of the DNS software (usually BIND, which originally stood for Berkeley Internet Name Domain).

- Placing the DNS server on a screened subnet of the firewall or router is sound practice.

- Limiting access to ports on this server to those required for functionality is often the key to avoiding compromise.

- DNS servers in the same domain must be able to transfer tables of information back and forth in a so-called "zone transfer." However, you do not want to allow systems outside your network to request this information, as it can enable an attacker to develop a more detailed picture of your internal network. Disallow all external zone transfers.

- The naming convention used for all assets outside of the common Internet servers such as World Wide Web (WWW) and e-mail should not be descriptive of an asset, making it easy for an intruder to figure out. A naming convention known only to the employees can often foil attackers.

Mail Servers

The mail server is the backbone of any electronic messaging environment. Mail servers are used as a communications hub and telephone directory for routing electronic messages from user to user over networks and the Internet. Mail servers are typically dedicated computers used to store and forward electronic messages to users who can receive messages through an enabled mail client. Although there are numerous vendors of mail server products, most require the UNIX or NT operating system. Some examples of the available messaging systems include MS Exchange and Lotus Notes.

Organizations can have one or more mail servers to service their user community. Typically, these servers use mail-specific protocols and messaging formats to shuffle information back and forth. The most common protocol between mail servers in TCP/IP networks is the Simple Mail Transfer Protocol (SMTP). SMTP is a "fire and forget" protocol that looks up the address of a recipient mail server and passes the mail to that destination. By itself, SMTP does not track the arrival and receipt of a message. However, many mail server/client products offer proof of arrival and receipt by embedding instructions that the mail client follows.

Another common protocol in mail systems is Post Office Protocol version 3 (POP3). This protocol is mainly used by clients retrieving mail from the mail server through a dialup connection. Mail servers support POP3 connections because the mail server can be configured to store messages for the client. The mail server essentially acts as the "Post Office" for the user. POP3 is inherently insecure, as it sends authentication information – user ID and password – in the clear. The APOP protocol – the A means Authenticated – is sometimes used as an alternative.

Mail servers both store and forward electronic messages to clients within a network. The content of the messages can be sensitive information that requires protection. For this reason, you should restrict both physical and network access to the mail server when deploying it on a network. The protection of a mail server over the network usually relies on settings within the operating system, and on restricted account access from remote locations. This is important to ensure the data stored in the mail server is protected, even after delivery. Security also must be provided for the backup tapes of the mail server – they too contain sensitive information.

Further, mail servers can hold sensitive information exchanged by users within the network and mailing lists of contact information. Failure to provide proper security for the physical and logical environments can result in exposure of sensitive electronic data on the user community. One concern with the storage and security of mailing lists in a user community is spam. Spam is the posting of irrelevant or inappropriate information to one or more mailing list of users within the network community. Spam is also called mail flooding and is often an intentional abuse of network resources.

Another concern is computer viruses. The mail server can contribute to Denial of Service (DoS) attacks through the intentional or unintentional circulation of computer viruses via electronic mail. A prime example of this type of threat was circulation of the Melissa virus, which used internal Outlook address lists to overburden and crash mail services. Another example was the "I Love You" virus that struck systems worldwide in May 2000.

When implementing a mail server, it is a good idea to place it in a location that provides some physical security and that restricts access to the machine. Another sound notion is to restrict logical connections to the server, with the exception of those required to route messages.

As a means of protecting sensitive information in the stored messages, some security mechanisms exist that allow the user community to encrypt electronic messages. One such mechanism is the Secure Multipurpose Internet Mail Extensions (S/MIME) messaging format. MIME is the most common format for encoding or formatting messages for transmittal in a messaging environment.

There are numerous commercial security products that can reduce spam, and scan messages for malicious content such as viruses, DoS attacks, and Trojan horses.

When implementing a mail server, an organization should consider the server software that is used, the platform required, and the external and internal security mechanisms necessary for the mail backbone. A short list of some of the security actions to take are:

- Establish a minimal number of restricted mail server administrator accounts. Those making policy and operational changes in the mail server should be required to do so only through local access to the server. This action reduces the chances that someone can break in with a virtual connection and perform malicious acts.

- Place the physical server in a location where you can restrict access to it, possibly even through login access. This action helps ensure that only authorized persons gain access to the machine.

- Implement a spam filtering software package on the mail server. Spam can overburden the mail server, making it crash, and the spam filtering software can minimize that risk.

- Put e-mail virus scanning software on the mail server. These software products usually have updates on new threats within 24 hours of a computer security incident. In addition, many vendors provide support through a Computer Security Incident Response Team (CSIRT). The CSIRT assists in fixing or undoing problems caused by malicious code such as viruses.

- Regularly change the passwords of the mail server administrative accounts to reduce risk from exhaustive password attacks or similar hacks. Alternately, for even greater security, use one-time passwords or tokens.

- Be sure to check for security advisories and to implement available patches when installing the mail server software.

- Ascertain if your software supports S/MIME, or some other security mechanism that can encrypt and protect the data stored on the file system. Another option is to perform a daily backup of the information contained in the mail server, removing the information from the file system. This provides some security from individuals accessing the mail server remotely and potentially tapping into sensitive data.

Web Servers

Web servers offer interactive services to customers and affiliates. They are one of the building blocks of e-Commerce. As such, additional care is required to maintain continuous service and protect the information exchanged. The communication between a Web server and a remote client using a Web browser typically is achieved through Hyper Text Transfer Protocol (HTTP). HTTP is considered an application level or layer protocol because the addressing and routing of HTTP requests is handled by TCP/IP. Using a Web browser, a Web client performs HTTP requests that contain the Uniform Resource Locator (URL) to retrieve network resources made available by a Web server or other network elements that support HTTP. Figure 3-16 shows typical scenario between a Web server and a Web client.

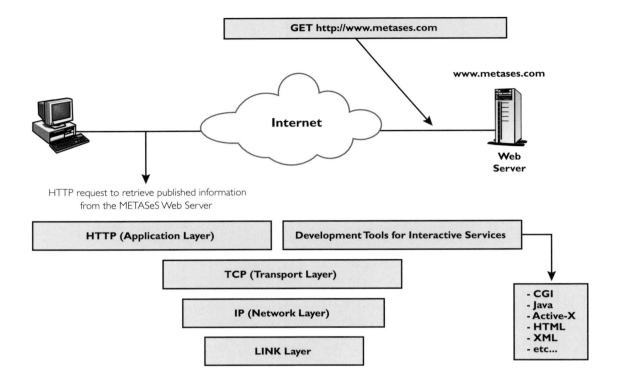

Figure 3-16: Web Server/Client Relationship

In addition to basic capabilities such as text presentation, Web servers can provide additional functionality by integrating multimedia applications.

A Web server may be placed in different topology configurations to accommodate the organizational needs for information exchange.

One scenario places the Web server in a Demilitarized Zone (DMZ), which is adjacent to a firewall. In the same network, there may be additional servers for such applications as e-mail or news. The DMZ configuration isolates network elements such as e-mail servers that, because they can be accessed from trustless networks, are exposed to external attacks. If one network element (for example, a Web server) is compromised, the configuration restricts the attacker's activities to the DMZ, because the firewall restricts traffic inbound to the internal network from the DMZ. Figure 3-17 depicts a DMZ configuration.

A second network configuration places the Web server inside the trusted network that is protected by a firewall (Figure 3-18). Any requests destined for the Web server are filtered at the firewall before they propagate to the internal network and finally reach the respective Web server.[7]

---

[7] It should be noted that, in both scenarios, the firewall or filtering device preceding the Web server is configured to allow only HTTP traffic on the specified ports where the Web server is accepting connections, typically ports 80, 443, or 8080. Other ports may be defined according to the Web server's configuration.

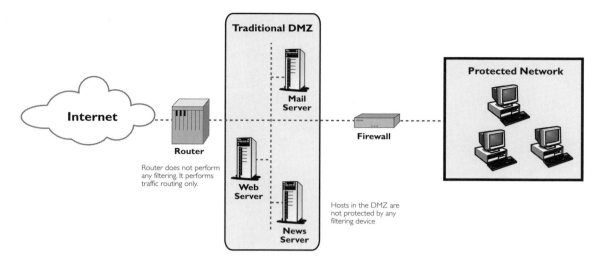

Figure 3-17: Web Server in DMZ Network

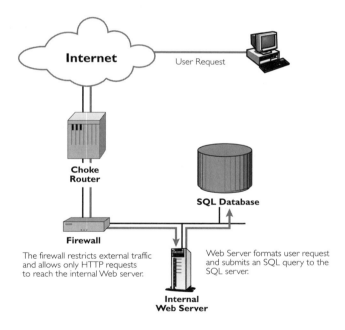

Figure 3-18: Web Server in Trusted Network

To protect against malicious attacks and ensure service of the Web server, some of the areas to examine are:

- **Traffic Load Analysis** – This provides insights into the sustainable capacity of the Web server or a Web farm of multiple Web servers. Capacity is how many transactions the server can sustain before performance degrades. This analysis ensures that the Web server can service requests without risk of service disruption due to traffic load. This is considered a form of Denial of Service (DoS) attack (a "self-inflicted" DoS), due not to malicious intent but lack of resources. Service disruption may translate to lost sales orders, frustrated customers, and consequent loss of revenue.

- **System to System Interaction** – Web servers that provide e-Commerce services or other interactive capabilities are often configured to interface with other internal or organizational affiliate systems (for example, a credit agency to verify a consumer's financial standing). The communication between the Web server and the remote system may be accomplished through a common application interface over a dial-up connection or over the Internet. An example is CGI scripts, which collect user input and submit SQL queries to the remote system for further processing.

  Any communication between the two systems must be authenticated using strong authentication mechanisms such as multi-factor authentication or S/Key, and performed over a secure channel. The secure channel must be able to sustain physical and logical attacks. Physical attacks may consist of eavesdropping on a physical medium such as coaxial cable, or destroying the physical medium. Logical attacks may consist of hacking the CGI script. In either case, consider protection mechanisms such as recovery, alternate routes, or point-to-point encryption at the link layer. In cases where the entire physical medium cannot be guaranteed protection – an example is a public switched network – you should enforce packet data encryption to protect against attacks such as traffic monitoring or session hijacking. Note that the encryption keys used by the encryption algorithm must be large enough (for example, 1024-bit length) to sustain cryptanalytic attacks.

- **System-to-User Interaction** – Two user communities pertain to this category: 1) external users such as customers or affiliates; and 2) internal users such a employees, system administrators, and Web developers. External user interaction consists of users on a network, such as the Internet, that is considered trustless. Internal user interaction consists of users, such as disgruntled employees, on a trusted network. Note that, in many organizations, traffic generated by people inside the network is more likely to be treated as "trusted" by devices such as routers or firewalls. Insiders, therefore, could cause a great deal more damage.

- **Malicious, Purposeful Attacks to Disrupt Service** – Also known as DoS attacks, these can be generated from external trustless networks or the internal network. Protection against these types of attacks require constant maintenance of the entire Web server. Maintenance includes monitoring and administering the health of the underlying operating system as well as additional applications or services supported by the Web server.

- **Attacks to Gain Unauthorized Access** – These are aimed at such objectives as defacing the Web site or, much more seriously, at using the Web server host as a launch pad to penetrate the internal network or other networks.

Both DoS attacks and attacks to gain unauthorized access attempt to exploit vulnerabilities with a particular service that is active on the Web server (for example, FTP, gopher, HTTP, or Telnet), or vulnerabilities in the underlying operating system (for example, TCP/IP stack implementation or authentication mechanisms). In addition, these attacks may be exercised on the Web server's interactive or multimedia services, which require the user to submit certain types of information. This information is captured through off-the-shelf applications or in-house developed applications, such as CGI scripts developed in various programming languages and HTML forms. The information is stored for further processing.

The vulnerabilities associated with interactive on-line applications are mostly based on poor configuration or run-time application errors that may allow an attacker to retrieve sensitive information from the Web server, or even compromise the security of the host. Poor configuration may consist of incorrect permissions for the files and directories that the application uses on the Web server, or incorrect application configuration settings that may affect the function of the application or even of the Web server itself. Run-time errors may include buffer overflows (and sometimes underflows), corrupted data, or inappropriate data input streams that the application cannot handle correctly.

To protect against such vulnerabilities, some of the actions you can take are to:

- Ensure that the underlying operating system maintains an adequate degree of security.

- Apply patches or service packs in a timely manner, especially when the patches attempt to mitigate security threats.

- Eliminate any services that do not aid in the general functionality of the host. Typically, only the HTTP service is accessible by trustless users or networks on a Web server.

- Remove all demo or test CGI scripts or other software from the server.

- Disallow all forms of networked file or volume sharing.

- Restrict Web server maintenance to specified administrators, and disallow any other login accounts.

- Carefully implement directory and file permissions to protect critical operating system files and Web server resources such as application or public directories.

- Enable auditing and logging and review periodically.

- Limit ownership of the Web server applications to non-privileged accounts. This eliminates threats of remote attacks that attempt to gain administrative privileges.

- Give ownership of the Web server process to a non-privileged account to eliminate attacks associated with the Web server daemon process.

- To eliminate threats such as information tampering, DoS, and disk space overflow, control the information storage and retrieval processes (for example, FTP and HTTP) by means of disk partitioning, file system permissions, and cryptographic signatures of critical files. By way of illustration, an attacker might use the anonymous FTP account to store illegal software copies, alter the contents of a file, or fill the hard disk to capacity to interrupt service.

- Restrict administration of the host and the Web server to authorized organizational personnel.

- Review the content of the information on the Web server to ensure that proprietary information is not disclosed.

- Inspect on-line applications that provide interactive services to end users (for example, sales orders and additional product information requests) where the user is required to supply input. Ensure that the applications can handle malicious attacks such as buffer overflows.

- Conduct periodic security assessments such as Web intrusion tests to detect vulnerabilities and to baseline the overall security posture.

Remote Access Servers

Remote access servers allow remote users to connect to organizational computing resources such as internal mail and data servers, or to act in effect as an ISP by providing Internet access. In a typical scenario, the remote access server allows remote and mobile users to dial up or connect through other network protocols such as TCP/IP, Point-to-Point Protocol (PPP), and Serial Line Support (SLIP), thus accessing internal organizational resources. (Figure 3-19). You can either connect to an access server from the Public Switched Telephone Network (PSTN) or the Internet to access internal resources.

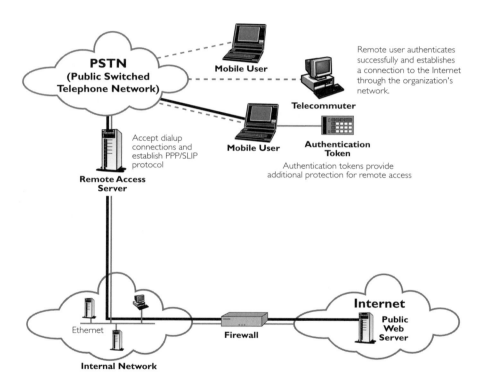

Figure 3-19: Remote Access Server & Mobile User Connection

Although helpful to mobile users, this method provides another avenue for intruders to attack and gain unauthorized access to an organization's internal resources. Attacks against the access server include DoS attacks, and attempts to exploit an existing vulnerability and gain unauthorized access. Thus, use extreme caution in the deployment and maintenance of the server operating software and hardware. To protect against attacks, some of the actions you might take are:

- Disable or remove all unnecessary services and protocols. Only keep activated those required for intended tasks such as connectivity, authentication, and encryption.

- Enable telephone number origination authentication to protect against war-dialing attacks (such as using dial back, caller Automatic number Identification, or similar verification methods).

- Change default administrative settings such as vendor-provided system passwords, and permissive access controls. One of the first ways in which intruders try to access a system is to take advantage of default configuration settings.

- Establish strong authentication mechanisms for remote users such as multi-factor authentication, or one-time password generators. Multi-factor authentication uses two or means of identifying a user to a system, such as something you know (a password or PIN) and something you have (a token).

- One-time passwords are a means of authenticating to a system using a password that is valid only once; each subsequent login requires a new password. One-time passwords can be generated a number of ways, including predetermined lists of pass phrases and time-synchronized devices.

- Enforce encryption during authentication and connection between the user and the remote access server to protect against network monitoring attacks.

- If remote administration is required to maintain the access server, encrypt all communications between it and the administrator's station.

- Provide redundancy and establish recovery procedures in the event of a natural disaster or DoS attack.

- Perform periodic assessments to ensure consistency of configuration settings.

Authentication Servers

Network and workstation operating systems support various forms of password-based authentication. In many cases, these static passwords are insecurely stored in a file on the system and can be discovered and exploited through a number of methods. Password-based authentication is susceptible to: 1) exhaustive password and/or dictionary attacks; 2) sniffing as the password data traverses the communication line; 3) simple discovery by people looking over your shoulder; and 4) in some cases, discovery by someone finding the locally stored password list. For these reasons, there is little assurance of security associated with password-based authentication. There are other authentication technologies that promise a higher level of assurance with your network and operating system access transactions.

Note that the general subject of authentication is discussed in the section Security Infrastructure and Services.

Many authentication systems rely on an external mechanism that not only generates one-time passwords for authenticating users, but provides the additional security of "something you have" plus "something you know," like having a bank card and a PIN. Such external mechanisms can be a physical token that the user possesses, like a smart card or PC card, or local client software, an algorithm calculator on the server, or a digital certificate. These external mechanisms correspond with an authentication database that resides at a known central location, such as on a server. The challenge mechanisms, actions, and ability of the authentication server depend on its implementation within a network.

The basic definition for an authentication server is a network device that challenges network entities, including computers and people, for their credentials to determine that they are who they claim to be. A user's credentials can be user name and password, a secret code, or any other data set that can be exclusively linked to a user and therefore used to establish the authenticity of that user. After a validated response to the authentication server challenge, the authentication server provides a certain assurance of the user's identity. Once the user has authenticated himself to the server, the server vouches for the identity of the user, and performs for the user network- or application-level login, or any other task relating to the user's authenticated identity.

There are several categories of authentication systems. Three of the most common types, with examples, are:

- **Single Sign-On** – (Unicenter TNG)
- **Token-Based** – (Axent Defender)
- **Digital Certificate-Based** – (Entrust, RSA)

Single Sign-On authentication is typically host-based. It requires users to authenticate to the server once, after which the server performs all other authentication seamlessly for the user. This type of server does not necessarily perform application-level authentication, although that implementation is possible. This server has an internal mapping table for each user that it services, and often refers to that table to provide the user access to specific information on or over the network. The credential challenge is usually a user name and static password, although many single sign-on products are beginning to provide support for digital certificate and/or token-based authentication.

Token-Based authentication uses a hardware- or software-based token that generates one-time use access codes that are known only by the server and the user. These secret access codes are usually valid for limited periods of time, after which the secret code expires and the user must generate a new code to authenticate. Token-based authentication is an example of an authentication system that vouches for the identity of users, because it provides some assurance beyond user name and password. A properly implemented token-based authentication system provides higher assurance that an individual is who he claims to be, and raises general network security by reducing vulnerability from the various password attacks and "over-the-shoulder surfing." Another security advantage is that session hijacking and sniffing become less effective attacks, since the token-generated passwords are single-use code.

However, token-based authentication is susceptible to "race" and "replay" attacks. In a "race" attack, a sniffing attacker watches as the user enters a pass code. His gambit is to make a good guess and try to "race" the user to the finish with the correct code. For example, say the user has entered the first nine digits of 10-digit numeric code. An attacker who sniffs out these first nine digits then has a 1 in 10 chance of guessing the correct tenth and final digit. A correct guess – entered before the legitimate user enters their tenth digit – grants the attacker access to the system. A "replay" attack is accomplished by recording a real act of authentication, and then "replaying" it to gain access. Setting time limits on the authentication data set, which is limited to one login (single use), can reduce vulnerability from these kind of attacks.

Digital Certificate-Based authentication servers are usually referred to a certificate authority. A certificate authority checks the validity of the digital signature by ensuring the validity of the signature of the trusted authority that issued the certificate. Then the identity of the user is established based on the content of the digital certificate. This type of authentication server vouches for the identity of the user through a third-party trust hierarchy. Certificates are generally used at the application level, although it is possible to implement a host-based system that uses certificates as the means of authentication.

A proper implementation of certificate authority and digital certificates can provide a high-trust environment that eliminates passwords and provides encrypted transmission throughout the network. This kind of environment would make password guessing and shoulder sniffing useless unless the digital certificate could be copied or taken. In addition, with the use of encrypted transmission of data, protection is provided against session hijacking and sniffing attacks.

Authentication servers can provide a high trust or single sign-on network environment. With a high-trust environment, authentication servers supply higher-assurance access control for applications and databases, ensuring that only the authenticated users gain access to them. With a single sign-on environment, users are seamlessly provided access to their authorized network utilities and applications. It is possible to provide a solution of both high trust and single signon through the use of high-assurance authentication systems.

The principal issue with all authentication servers is trust. The authentication server should be the most trusted network device. The trust associated with the authentication server is directly related to the level of assurance that is gained by the network. If the authentication server is vulnerable, the level of trust gained through authentication with the server is rendered moot. In the event that the authentication server is used as a single sign-on solution, this point is doubly important, since the authentication server becomes a single point of failure or security compromise for the network. Assurances must exist that the authentication server is impregnable so that network access cannot be improperly gained and abused by anyone that penetrates security controls.

Implementation of an authentication server can require major infrastructure changes, depending on the type of authentication and the reason for it. Regardless of the level of assurance you are seeking, planning, implementation, and management of authentication services requires experience and expertise. To reemphasize, it is imperative that, when planning for an authentication server, you identify the server as the most secure and trusted network component. Failure to do so could result in a false sense of security and provide authentication to untrusted individuals.

When implementing an authentication server, some of the steps you might take are:

- Analyze the effects of its deployment on the existing network. Factor in the cost of changes, if any, to the existing network to determine the feasibility of an authentication server.

- Identify the level of assurance desired for the network, and compare that level of assurance with those provided by the selected product. Ensure that the methods used for credential challenge provide you with sufficient assurance of the identity of the individuals using the server services.

- Identify the logical location of your authentication system. If you intend to use the services of the authentication system for your internal network only, place the authentication server behind an internal firewall or secure gateway to limit network-wide access. For implementations intended for internal and external authentication, ensure that the security of the authentication systems (and supporting components) are adequate to resist attacks from unknown entities in the external environment.

- Place the server in a physical location where you can restrict access and, possibly, even log access to it. This helps ensure that only authorized persons gain access to the machine.

- Use one-time passwords for the administrative accounts on your authentication servers. This provides some protection from dictionary and exhaustive password attacks performed on the server.

- Enforce two-person integrity for all changes that need to be made to the internal policies of the authentication server, to ensure that no single person has the ability to compromise its integrity.

- Be sure to check for security advisories, and implement any security patches necessary to secure the authentication server.

- Ensure that sensitive information stored in internal tables, such as passwords or access codes for single sign-on environments, are not easily accessible. Encrypt them or place them in a secure database that requires administrative access.

- Make one secure backup of the authentication server, and lock the media in a media-rated safe. Safes designed to store documents do not protect magnetic media.

- To identify the vulnerabilities to potential authentication server products, apply findings from independent security assessments.

- Perform a full security assessment of your environment with the implemented authentication server product. Attempt to penetrate the security of the environment and access sensitive information by capturing plain text communications, hacking the authentication server, and hijacking user sessions.

X.500/Lightweight Directory Access Protocol (LDAP)-based Directory Services

A directory is a repository of related information such as a list of telephone numbers. Directory services provide a mechanism for accessing information within the directory. Presently, the *de facto* standard for client-to-directory access is the Lightweight Directory Access Protocol (LDAP), derived from the X.500 Directory Access Protocol. Typically, directories are centrally located, providing the user community and directory-enabled applications, devices, and systems with a single convergence point of information. Sharing similar qualities with traditional database applications, directories can be thought of as specialized databases optimized for read performance. Vendor-specific implementations of directory services include Microsoft Active Directory and Novell NDS.

Modern-day directories are at the center of emerging security architectures. The role of directories has been extended beyond being a mere collection of user information. User attributes other than name and telephone numbers, including digital certificates, authentication parameters, and authorization permissions, are being incorporated in a directory. Also contained within a directory are security and management attributes for devices and systems that support the network infrastructure, such as routers, firewalls, and file servers. Reliability, availability, and scalability become serious issues if a central directory is the focal point for security information. A malfunctioning or poorly configured directory server could potentially cripple an organization.

Once security information is centralized, you can develop applications that look to the directory for user-specific information. This makes the directory a central point for applying corporate-wide security policy, and eliminates the need for application-specific user account databases. Granted, application-specific attributes may still need to be tracked by individual applications or systems. However, centralized user management concentrates and simplifies the execution of functions. For example, if the directory denies access to a terminated employee, every other application, device, and system knows the employee has been terminated.

While the idea of centralized security management is certainly attractive, achieving such a goal is much more difficult than simply installing a directory. Critical areas to consider when implementing directory services include:

- Be sure to specifically enable the large majority of applications, devices, and systems currently in use to make effective use of directory services.

- Exercise great care with the type of information in the directory and the type and amount of access granted to it. Inadequate access controls, for example, could expose password or personal information to any requestor. Similarly, storing sensitive information in plain – or even encrypted – text within the directory may make the directory an attractive target for an attacker.

Servers/Operating Systems (OS)

Servers provide many services to end users, from processing housing applications to data storage. Servers provide the underlying infrastructure for establishing data and application management for an organization. Possible attacks include DoS and service fraud. Therefore, take steps such as the following to ensure adequate security:

- Deploy strong authentication procedures (hardware or software tokens).

- Enforce data encryption to protect sensitive data. Configure the server to provide encryption of the data transmitted across the network, or provide underlying network protocols that can support data encryption.

- Offer security training to the administrators that manage the server and its applications.

- Replicate the production server to establish a test server to test the manufacturer's new releases and updates.

- Establish an organizational policy that specifies the rules for proper interaction with the server's applications or data, and spells out the consequences if such interaction is abused.

- Establish documentation for configuring the security of the operating system and related services such as TCP/IP, remote access servers, and modems.

- Perform penetration tests to identify vulnerabilities.

- Establish disaster recovery procedures.

Desktops/Operating Systems (OS)

This section addresses security issues associated with the general aspects, such as the operating system and e-mail, of the end user's desktop environment.

Operating Systems

An operating system is the underlying component of the end user's desktop that enables the execution of higher-level applications on behalf of the operating user. Every commercial operating system has vulnerabilities that attackers can exploit to gain unauthorized access. Among the major issues you should concern yourself with are vulnerabilities, default configuration, and user education. To improve security, take steps such as the following:

- Draw up an organizational policy to address misuse of the computing platform and to specify the consequences of misuse.

- Educate users on operating system security, such as file and directory permissions, sound password selection, and operating system updates and patches.

- Establish documentation for configuring the security of the operating system.

- Provide strong authentication mechanisms such as tokens.

- Perform regular, comprehensive network penetration assessments to identify desktop vulnerabilities.

- Send desktop users both alerts and mitigation strategies on high-impact vulnerabilities. This helps protect mobile users who are not directly connected to the organization's network, and who thus cannot automatically update their software through push or pull[8] technology.

E-Mail

E-mail is a major communication channel. As such, it becomes a target for misuse or a tool for performing malicious acts originated internally or externally. These acts include e-mail spamming, message monitoring, and virus or Trojan program propagation. To protect against these kind of attacks, some of the actions you can take include:

- Provide encryption and digital signing capabilities to e-mail clients to protect message transmission.

- Educate users about recognizing malicious e-mail attachments and suspicious e-mail messages before attempting to open them.

- Ensure that a policy outlines the proper use of e-mail and the consequences of violating the policy.

- Establish antiviral software, either on the e-mail server or the client, that can inspect e-mail content and attachments. Typically, e-mail servers are equipped with such software, but organizations should supply it to telecommuters or mobile users as well.

Browsers

Web browsers can retrieve on-line content published internally by the organization or on external Web sites. Since the inception of HTML, there have been a plethora of Web site services and delivery formats that require the end user to have a compliant browser to retrieve

---

[8] Some organizations automatically "push" new updates to end-user desktops.

multimedia content. This content may require the installation of, for example, a new plug-in or the enabling of Java on the Web browser. Multimedia content is an attractive method for presenting and receiving information. However, it poses its own kind of security threats associated with multimedia services such as ActiveX, Java, and HTML, particularly in regard to hidden elements. Intruders can employ these tools to access the user's desktop and collect information.

Some of the measures to protect against browser-related attacks include:

- Enforce filtering mechanisms that restrict visits to sites unrelated to the organization's operations or business, and that restrict the execution of JavaScript, Java, or ActiveX code.

- Educate users about threats associated with on-line browsing such as disclosure of organizational or personal information. Establish an organizational policy that outlines the proper use of Web browsers and online resources.

Security Infrastructure and Services

Certain security infrastructure and services elements are incorporated in a typical e-Commerce application. They include:

- Authentication
- Firewalls
- Virtual Private Networks (VPNs)
- Encryption
- Virus scanning
- Intrusion Detection Systems (IDS)

Each element is discussed in the sections that follow.

Authentication

Authentication is a fundamental tenet of security. Authentication is the process or ability to identify a person, resource, or system that is requesting access to another person, resource, or system. It has become a daily routine of our work and private lives, something we all do whenever we present an ATM card and PIN, or log into a corporate network with a user ID and password. Similarly, authentication is an integral part of using the Internet, whether it involves a user ID and password-protected ISP connection, or the digital certificates presented by Web sites when you establish an SSL-encrypted Internet session.

The ability to accurately authenticate users is of paramount importance to an overall security infrastructure. Without it, even the strongest security measures are rendered irrelevant as one user can easily assume the identity of any other. That "other user" could easily be the CEO or the system administrator with unrestricted privileges or access to sensitive data. Even firewalls, SSL sessions, and IP address-based security measures are made ineffectual without the ability to authenticate users and resources.

Put simply, there are four general classifications of authentication mechanisms. These mechanisms, and examples for each, are:

1. Something you know (a password or PIN number).

2. Something you have (a smart card, ATM card, or other token).

3. Something you are (biometrics such as a fingerprint or retinal scan).

4. Something you do (behavior such as the way in which you sign your name).

For lower-assurance applications, "something you know" such as user IDs and passwords may provide adequate authentication. For higher-assurance applications, "something you have" such as a token may be necessary. In cases where strong – or stronger – authentication is required, it may be appropriate to use several classes of authentication mechanisms simultaneously. This is known as multi-factor authentication.

It is extremely important to identify the resources you wish to protect and determine the appropriate level of assurance required for those resources. Once defined, authentication practices that are documented, uniform, and secure must be employed and adhered to by your user community.

The following are some issues to consider when establishing authentication requirements:

- Define what is being protected and how much it is worth; these answers dictate appropriate assurance levels. Passwords alone may be sufficient for authorizing, say, $10 transactions. However, passwords are likely inappropriate for authorizing a $1,000,000 transaction.

- When using smart cards or other physical tokens, analyze the business impact if a user loses or forgets her token. Establish procedures to minimize the impact of this.

- Educate users on appropriate password protection policies, and why actions such as leaving passwords in plain view are bad. Education is key; simply telling users not to do something is ineffective. Instruct them on the risks involved.

Firewalls

A firewall is a hardware platform combined with specialized software or firmware that protects the resources of a private network from users on other networks. Firewalls are typically deployed at Internet gateways, but they may also be used within an enterprise network to separate network segments with differing security requirements, or on dedicated links between two enterprise networks. There are two kinds of firewalls: 1) packet screening; and 2) application proxy.

Packet screening firewalls themselves have two types: static filtering , and dynamic or stateful filtering. The first uses static information about the connection to determine whether or not it is allowed to pass packet datagrams. The second records dynamic information about the network connection for the data that is leaving the protected network. It requires the returning network packets to exhibit the same dynamic information before being allowed back through the firewall.

Application proxies are packaged with many firewalls. They receive requests from the inside of the network that are destined for external resources, or *vice versa*. Once it receives a request, a proxy sends it to the outside networks as if it had originated at the firewall. Each proxy is typically written to support a specific protocol, allowing proxies in many cases to discern between valid protocol data and an attack.

At the most basic level, a router with enabled packet filters meets the definition of a firewall. Most commercial firewalls offer considerably more features, including threat monitoring, traffic rules, and even configurations customized to particular incoming user IDs or activity patterns. Many firewalls also include Virtual Private Network (VPN) capability. It is important to determine your needs and requirements, and then find a vendor who offers a firewall that fulfills your criteria.

In their role as gateway guardians, firewalls are often one of the first targets for anyone attacking a network from the Internet. Firewalls that have not been properly configured or maintained can be subverted or compromised such that they allow undesirable traffic to traverse the logical perimeter. You should note that more firewalls have fallen to configuration errors than to design flaws.

It's very important, therefore, to establish documented, uniform, and secure practices for configuring and maintaining firewalls on your organization's network. Many of the considerations for installing and configuring routers also apply to firewalls, given the similarity of the methods used by both. (See the section Routers.)

Among the additional issues to consider are:

- When installing a new firewall, check that the operating system on which the firewall software runs is properly secured, and that all non-essential services have been eliminated.

- If the firewall is to be monitored through use of Simple Network Management Protocol (SNMP), it is good practice to configure your firewall only to send traps (that is, alert, status, or control messages) rather than receive them. Thus, the firewall can only send out information data, and its state cannot be altered on the fly by incoming SNMP messages. Configuring firewalls to ignore incoming SNMP messages also provides protection in cases where default SNMP community strings (that is, passwords) have not been changed, and thus could be hacked, or where vendors have implemented hidden and undocumented community strings.

- Test firewall rule sets in a controlled environment, using a network monitor to ensure that the rules you set down are being implemented as intended. For example, you want to confirm that the traffic you intended to block is, in fact, being blocked.

- Make firewall rule sets very concise; they should only reflect the traffic that is allowed in either direction.

- The very last and most important rule should always be "Deny All" – deny any traffic that is not explicitly allowed.

Often the firewall is the only device on the perimeter, after the border router, that belongs to the network. While it may be tempting to place services such as the World Wide Web (WWW) on this same platform, a better solution is to use Network Address Translation (NAT). NAT allows you to specify that any connections bound for the WWW port on the outside of your firewall are directed to an actual Web server on the inside, while at the same time denying access to any other resources on that WWW machine.

Location of the Domain Name Service (DNS) server in respect to the firewall is often a perplexing problem. If you wish to place your DNS server outside the firewall, then you must develop a rule limiting internal DNS requests only to the external DNS server, and likewise limiting incoming DNS traffic from your external DNS server. A common problem occurs when a rule is defined letting into the network any traffic that originates from the DNS port on any machine. This allows attackers to make all traffic appear as if it is originating from their DNS port.

In another vein, a very important part of managing a firewall is maintaining logs. Logs can provide a record of all traffic that has been allowed or denied, as well as many firewall-specific tasks. A log may also contain utilization data such as employees' most frequently visited Web sites. For these reasons, regularly replacing log files and backing up the old logs is important. Backing up should be a manual process, or performed by software developed solely for that purpose. Do not use generic network backup software, as crackers can readily hack into it.

Lastly, firewalls often need to be managed remotely. The remote locations should originate from within the internal network. Most firewall software supports an encrypted channel between the firewall and a remote monitoring console.

Virtual Private Networks (VPNs)

A Virtual Private Network (VPN) is a network that is distributed across public networks, yet provides integrity, confidentiality, and in many cases authenticity of the data transmitted across public lines, thus making the distributed network seem private. VPNs are essentially encrypted network connections that allow computers to transmit data across the Internet or some other public network while ensuring that the data is not publicly available to others using that shared public resource network. VPNs are designed to make distributed networks look and feel like private trusted environments. They provide administrators and engineers of the internal networks assurances that the data being transmitted over public wires is protected, just as if it were data passed on internal network lines.

Through VPN technology, companies expect to reduce the cost incurred through leased dedicated lines by using local Point of Presence (POP) entities, such as Internet Service Providers (ISPs). This use of POP provides cost savings from leased lines. It also provides some fault tolerance, as sites are connected directly to one another as opposed to being connected over one shared line. In addition, VPNs are intended to raise the company's security level and integrate remote users tightly into the network, an option that isn't always available or cost-effective with leased lines.

Trusted and Untrusted VPNs

VPNs can be trusted or untrusted, depending on their design and implementation. Untrusted VPNs only provide the services of encrypted tunnels from one point to another, thus connecting all the network pockets together into a distributed yet secluded environment. An example of this type of VPN would be a network of five locations connected with router encrypted tunnels. The data flowing from any one of the five locations would be protected as it was transmitted to its destination. In many ways, SSL-encrypted Web sessions where users do not need to authenticate themselves to establish the SSL session can be thought of as an untrusted VPN. At best, access can be limited based upon the location of the IP address where the untrusted VPN connection originates.

Trusted VPNs encrypt data, just as untrusted VPNs can, but provide more "granularity," by challenging the user to authenticate to the VPN gateway. (Granularity is the use of more precise, "finer-grained" means of allowing or blocking access.) Once authenticated, granular access controls can be enforced through policy settings that dictate what the user can and cannot do. A primary difference between trusted and untrusted VPNs is that an untrusted VPN does not know who is sending data through its tunnel, whereas a trusted VPN establishes the identity of its service users.

Due to advanced encryption practices, the information transmitted across a VPN tunnel may not be susceptible to compromise. Note however, that does not imply that the data transmitted is trusted data.

Access controls must be used to ensure that only authorized network users have access to the VPN services. Access to the tunnels have to be allowed only from the internal network. The level of trust in the information transmitted over VPN tunnels is directly related to the level of assurance in the authentication mechanisms of the access controls. A sound practice is to analyze the authentication methodology and access controls to ensure that unauthorized, public domain users cannot access the VPN. These points are doubly important with trusted VPNs. When using trusted VPNs, there is usually an attitude of trust and "non-repudiation" – often misplaced – toward the data. Still, there are VPNs that do provide evidentiary services that establish non-repudiation and heightened trust in the data. These trusted VPN models typically use digital certificates in a managed certificate environment.

VPN Gateways

The end points of a VPN are called VPN gateways. A VPN gateway is essentially a secure router that communicates with the destination network. A VPN gateway usually communicates with another VPN gateway or a VPN client that serves as a gateway for a user.

The traffic over the VPN is only as secure as its end points. Failure to secure either end can result in a hole in your network infrastructure. For example: Company A and Company B have an encrypted link between them over the Internet. If someone breaks into Company A (end point one), then he can use its VPN to attack Company B (end point two).

A complication of VPNs is transmission of data either through or around a firewall. Because the tunnels are encrypted, the firewall that protects your internal network from a public one may not be able to filter packets, or ensure that incoming traffic does not damage your internal network (for example, through viruses, DoS attacks, exhaustive password attacks, etc.). You must be sure that your firewall can analyze the data coming through the VPN gateway, and that only trusted individuals and secure computers have access to the VPN tunnel. It is a good idea to restrict VPN traffic to specified ports, to reduce the chances of attack from the public domain.

Failure to properly implement a VPN gateway can open up your internal networks to the public domain, expose transmitted data to compromise from it, or even reduce the ability of your firewall to protect your internal network. In addition, the creation and tearing down of too many VPN sessions with a trusted VPN – for example, 10,000 simultaneous sessions – can burden a VPN gateway to the point where internal users experience a DoS.

In summary, implementation of VPNs is a major change to network infrastructures. Experience and expertise are required to plan, implement, and manage them. When mapping out a VPN solution, it is crucial you identify and document your business requirements and select a product that meets or exceeds those requirements.

Among the other important steps you might take are:

- Consider the effect of a VPN's implementation on the existing network. It is a good idea to factor in the cost of changes, if any, to the existing network to determine the feasibility of a VPN solution.

- Put into place authentication mechanisms for VPN gateways. These are crucial to the successful implementation of the VPN. In the event of weak authentication mechanisms, the data may be protected, but the weakest link becomes the VPN gateway, and the trust associated with the exchanged information is reduced. In addition, thoroughly test the access control mechanisms to ensure that external, unauthorized individuals cannot access your internal network.

- Ensure that the VPN solution you choose is a scalable product that can grow as your network or budget grows.

- Verify that the VPN solution is interoperable with similar network solutions. Failure to do so could entail an expensive re-engineering of the infrastructure.

- Ensure that the VPN solution supports and complies with industry standards, such as IPSec. IPSec is recommended by the Internet Engineering Task Force (IETF) for IP-level security. Products that adhere to standards are more likely to interoperate with related or similar products. Many of today's VPN products support ISAKMP, Oakley, or similar protocol frameworks to protect the data streamed through the open VPN session. The IPSec-recommended standard provides a road map for cross-protocol exchange that allows VPNs and similar technologies of differing frameworks to interoperate.

- Consider the manageability of the VPN. Evaluate whether the credentials of users require extensive management, or if the VPN software automates the management process.

- Ensure that the encryption algorithms for the encrypted tunnel are strong enough to provide adequate data protection. Moreover, look for products, such as such as L2TP, that support standardized encryption protocols.

Encryption

Like authentication, confidentiality is another fundamental security tenet. Encryption is an enabler of confidentiality. Sensitive information can be scrambled to render it effectively unintelligible to all but the intended recipient. Once received, the recipient can unscramble or decrypt the message. Without encryption, it is impossible to protect sensitive information such as e-mail messages, passwords, and credit card numbers from observation as it traverses the Internet or your corporate network. Encryption can also be an enabler of authentication: digital certificates, digital signatures, and the larger Public Key Infrastructure (PKI) applications rely upon encryption.

Like many technologies, encryption can be detrimental when applied inappropriately. Simply using encryption does not necessarily make a message or application secure. Inventing unproven or home-grown encryption algorithms, using weak encryption keys, or even using the right encryption in the wrong place can lull an organization into a false sense of security. Further, relying solely upon encryption for security instead of shoring up other deficiencies can lead to greater security risks. An example of this would be using 128-bit SSL encrypted connections between customers and the Web server, but not securing the backend database containing 300,000 credit card numbers. In this example, the backend aggregate database is a far more attractive target than individual customers.

Some of the considerations for using encryption include:

- When selecting the bit length ("bit strength") of an encryption algorithm, consider how long you need to protect the information. Information that needs to be kept secret for, say, one hour has very different strength requirements than information that needs to be kept secret for ten years. Less strong encryption algorithms can be selected for protecting the data for only one hour, so long as the chosen algorithm takes – and will take in the foreseeable future – greater than one hour to break.

- When encrypted data needs to be kept for a long time, be certain to have a key management and data recovery procedure in place in the event that encryption keys are compromised, the person holding the encryption keys quits, etc. This is particularly important in PKI, as a user's credentials have a finite lifetime. Once those credentials expire and are replaced, any information encrypted using those credentials is no longer accessible unless there is a key management and recovery plan.

Virus Scanning

Virus scanning has been an important safeguard in most organizations' security infrastructure for years. Traditionally, virus scanning was performed at each user's desktop, and automatically scanned files in the background as they were accessed. If a virus was found, execution of the infected program or loading of the infected document was halted, and an attempt was made at disinfecting the file. As the world has become more connected through the Internet and internal networks, virus scanning functionality was extended to devices such as firewalls, file servers, and mail servers.

Scanning at the network perimeter or other aggregation point, such as a mail server, is an organization's first line of defense. Desktop virus scanning catches viruses missed at the perimeter, or introduced at the desktop via floppy disk or encrypted mail messages.

Scanning for viruses at the network perimeter can severely curtail the potential damage inflicted upon an organization. For example, despite widespread and numerous warnings about the "I Love You" virus, many people still launched the virulent e-mail attachment. Desktop virus scanners that were not updated – or were not running in the first place – allowed these users to be infected with, and contribute to, the spread of the virus. Employing an up-to-date virus scanner at the network perimeter or on a central mail server can eliminate many such desktop infections.

In addition to scanning for viruses at the perimeter and desktop, modern virus scanners can also be configured to alert a central entity within an organization if a virus is detected. These alerts can potentially act as an advance warning mechanism of potential risks. Such mechanisms, combined with automated virus signature updates, can greatly reduce the risk of viral infection.

Some key considerations for deploying virus scanning as a component of a security infrastructure include:

- Consider selecting virus scanning products from different vendors for scanning at the network perimeter and at user desktops. Although each vendor's virus scanning package supports substantially the same virus signatures, there are differences in techniques, the speed and frequency of virus signature updates, and the total number of viruses detected. Using products from multiple vendors increases the likelihood of detecting a virus.

- Virus scanning on firewalls themselves is typically a poor idea due to security and performance concerns. Instead, offload the virus scanning functions to another system, using technologies such as Content Vectoring Protocol (CVP).

- Consider purchasing virus scanning software for your users' home computers in addition to their office and/or laptop computers. This is critical if those users have remote access to your corporate network.

Intrusion Detection System (IDS)

An Intrusion Detection System (IDS) detects anomalies that may indicate malicious activity on a network or network device. The two common types of IDS are network and host-based. The network IDS examines network traffic for malicious activity, while the host-based IDS monitors several elements of the particular operating system it supports.

The common IDS network architecture is composed of two types of devices. The first device, of which there may be many, collects data and is commonly referred to as the "engine" or "sensor." The second device, of which there is commonly only one, manages the engine and is referred to as the "console" or "data repository." Both the sensor and the console normally run on an Intel- or SPARC- based platform.

The bulk of the work is done on the sensor, where the traffic is actually examined and subsequently flagged or ignored. This determination is accomplished through filters, attack signatures recognition, and other security elements.

The console usually stores the data after it is collected from the sensor. Policies to determine what to monitor for are developed there and "pushed" out to the sensors. Reporting is also normally a console function – alerts that the sensors generate are sent there for scrutiny. Optimally, there are many sensors to one console, which allows distributed management.

Appropriate configuration is very important when deploying an IDS. Typically, an IDS is deployed in as passive a way as possible to help prevent detection of the IDS on the network. When an IDS is configured to only "listen," it is then not accessible from the network being monitored by the IDS.

When deciding how to position a network-based IDS sensor on a perimeter network, it is important to understand your deployment goals. Depending on the amount of traffic on the monitored wire, it may be a good idea to simply monitor inbound attacks. This can be accomplished with careful filter development (see below). Commonly, an IDS is designed to protect the corporation from malicious users who are either internal and external to the network. The question to ask might be, "Which do we wish to protect: our network from the Internet or the Internet from our network?" If downstream legal liability is a concern, then it may be appropriate to add another IDS sensor to the perimeter. Each sensor will have its own name and IP address. This makes it easier to determine from which side of the network an attack is occurring.

While deploying an IDS is an exercise in network architecture, developing the policies for the IDS is quite similar to developing the policies for a firewall or router (see the section Firewalls and the section Routers).

Some of the additional elements and considerations are:

- **Filters** – Normally, filters designate traffic that the network-based IDS should not examine. Many times, these filters actually optimize the IDS by allowing it to focus cycles on only the important traffic. These filters usually are defined by IP addresses, netmask, protocol, and port. To develop a good set of filters, it is important to become familiar with the topology of the network in question.

- **Attack Signatures** – IDS software is commonly shipped with a database of known attack signatures. This is a collection, developed by the IDS vendor, of the identifying characteristics of various known network attacks, such as viruses, against which collected traffic is compared. Many of these signatures may be irrelevant to the network being monitored, and may be safely turned off. For instance, if it is known that there are no POP servers on the monitored network, not performing this check helps optimize the IDS.

- **Connection-Based Event Collection** – This aspect of the network-based IDS allows the user to specify network events that are deemed important, yet which are not associated with known attacks. These rules are commonly defined by IP addresses, netmask, protocol, and port. They are very similar to the rules designated for filters, and are defined in much the same way. An example would be to flag all traffic as high priority that originates from the Internet, and is a TCP packet destined for port 23 on any devices associated with the network. In this example, you flag anyone using Telnet to access your assets from an untrusted network.

Determining who is responsible for the day-to-day configuration and monitoring of the IDS is important. The personnel responsible for the IDS should be highly trustworthy, and few in number. Audit trails are highly recommended to determine what changes are made and where. Keep in mind that this is not another functional element of the network, but is akin to a burglar alarm.

You should develop a policy that delineates the steps to take in the event of a detected intrusion. Several factors weigh into this policy. How many people, for example, should be made aware of an intrusion? How can the intrusion be stopped? It may be possible to stop it through router logs or a firewall update. These types of questions should be answered before deploying your IDS infrastructure.

Conclusion

This chapter covered the key elements of building secure Web and e-Commerce systems. The above survey of various technologies, which make up the key infrastructure underpinnings of e-Commerce systems, should help you better understand each component from a security perspective. Our goal was to provide you with basic understanding of the building blocks of a secure system, and to provide a set of pragmatic best practices in developing system-level security architectures and in infusing security into the system development life cycle (SDLC) processes. Both are vital to the end goal – creating systems that appropriately meet the security requirements of the business.

For those of you with a technical appetite, we hope we were able to satiate it in chapter 3. However, we feel compelled to mention – yet again – that the technology is only one of four other major security program elements, along with organization, process, and policies, standards, and procedures. And in fact, even system-level security architecture pertains to both technical and non-technical controls. So we've devised the following Top Five list as our parting bit of summary wisdom. If asked to implement a best practice Information Security Program at your organization, we would stress the following key points:

1. Pay attention to the broader program as well as the individual systems. Since security is the quintessential example of the "weakest link" theory, even perfect security technology is no guarantee of security.

2. Sweat the "people" details. Some of the best risk reduction payback is the result of providing training and awareness programs and of documenting processes and procedures.

3. "Eat the elephant" one bite at a time. Since there is likely much to do, creating a pragmatic, well prioritized plan with achievable goals is critical.

4. Make sure that business tie-ins are always present. Whether you are focusing on specific system-level security architecture, or the overall security program, be certain the business requirements are front and center in the discussion and the solution. Despite security's increased importance to business, and even the trend toward more spending on security that we have noted, at the end of the day organizations view Information Security as an overhead cost.

   One factor makes the business tie-in even more important. Since security is a long-term project (a journey, not a destination), attaining and maintaining the appropriate funding level is as important as gaining the initial budget. If you cannot tie funding requests to business goals, you will have a serious uphill climb ahead of you.

5. Have some fun! Let's face it: many security professionals tend toward the paranoid side of things. But Information Security is one of the most exciting areas in the technology scene, and it will be for some time. Because Information Security is really largely about behavior modification, you will get superior results with the sugar-versus-vinegar approach.

Appendix A:
Excerpt from a Sample
Information Security Gap Analysis

This report documents the results of a information security "Gap Analysis" performed by METASeS for WeProduceIt.com (WPI.com). WPI.com is a manufacturer with headquarters in Anytown, USA.

WPI.com contracted with METASeS for a focused information security assessment to determine how the company's information security program compared with industry and METASeS best practices. As part of the overall program assessment, METASeS performed the Gap Analysis against our best practices in the following four program areas:

1. Policy Framework (i.e., Policies, Standards, and Procedures)
2. Organization
3. Technology
4. Process

WPI.com asked that METASeS apply its pioneering service methodologies to conduct the analysis. In addition, WPI.com specifically asked that METASeS focus on the security aspects of WPI.com's Internet and Partner Network access.

As shown in Figure A-1, the METASeS Gap Analysis methodology follows a traceable progression from data collection and analysis through development of recommendations for improving the program. Additional details of the METASeS methodology are presented in Section 2.

From an overall standpoint, the information security program at WPI.com is below industry norms as determined by METASeS.

METASeS uses key findings descriptors to support quick review of assessment results. The descriptors are described in Figure A-2.

The **Best Practice** category is reserved for those security approaches that are consistent with METASeS best practices. The Best Practice category does not suggest that the organization has done everything possible to implement a viable information security program. Rather, METASeS recommends these best practices as the most consistently cost effective means of implementing information security measures in a specific program area.

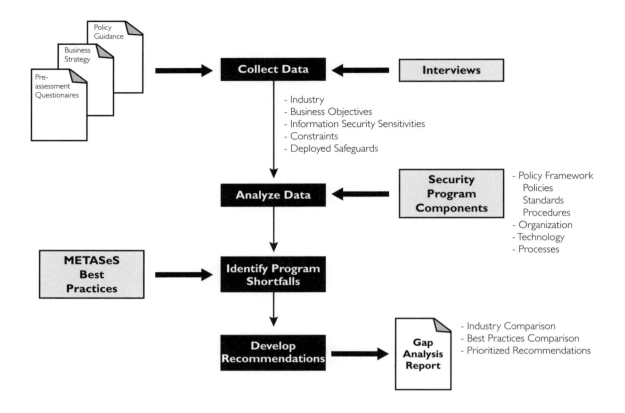

Figure A-1: METASeS Gap Analysis Methodology

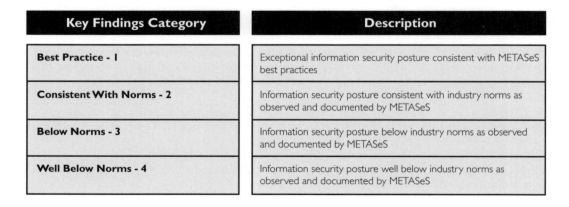

Key Findings Category	Description
Best Practice - 1	Exceptional information security posture consistent with METASeS best practices
Consistent With Norms - 2	Information security posture consistent with industry norms as observed and documented by METASeS
Below Norms - 3	Information security posture below industry norms as observed and documented by METASeS
Well Below Norms - 4	Information security posture well below industry norms as observed and documented by METASeS

Figure A-2: Key Findings Descriptors

The **Consistent With Norms** category is for those security approaches that are consistent with industry norms as observed and documented by METASeS. METASeS information security specialists have considerable experience in assessing the information security posture of companies in a wide range of industries. This METASeS knowledge base allows us to determine which information security practices are consistent with the norms for a given industry (or generally consistent with our findings at other similar customers). Findings in this category do not suggest that the information security posture is necessarily acceptable. Often, industry norms reflect a general shortfall in industry understanding or appropriate treatment of a specific program area. The **Below Norms** and **Well Below Norms** categories are for those security approaches that reflect moderate and significant shortfalls as compared to industry norms.

The same four categories shown in Figure A-2 also are used to describe the individual factors that contributed to the key findings. Figure A-3 summarizes the METASeS assessment of the information security program at WPI.com for the four program areas.

Assessment Perspective	Summary Finding	Contributing Factors
Policy Framework	Best Practice	• Established some key policies. • Missing some key policies (e.g., Asset Classification and Acceptable Use) • No technical standards (e.g., System and Network Configuration). • Very few well-defined procedures.
Organization	Consistent with Norms	• Organization structure is missing a single point of ownership for information security (i.e., there is no Chief Information Security Officer). • No clearly defined organizational interfaces to key IT departments and processes (e.g., application development, change management, etc.).
Technology	Below Norms	• Screening routers and commercial firewall systems implemented. • Some key servers (e.g., HR_Server) placed on subnets accessible by personnel with no need for access. • No configuration monitoring solution (e.g., ISS S3, AXENT Enterprise Security Manager, etc.) implemented to maintain company-standard configurations. • Modems implemented through secured modem pool. • Discovered some unauthorized modems. • Implemented intrusion detection system pilot.
Processes	Well Below Noms	• No formal information security training program for security staff. • No security awareness training for end users. • No defined risk assessment process. • No formal security architecture review process.

Figure A-3: Summary Findings in Each Program Area

Analysis Summary

As a national telecommunications provider, WPI.com is highly reliant on secure, reliable information systems to meet the company's primary business objectives of:

- Increasing the company's market share by at least 3 percent per year.
- Achieving and maintaining end-to-end network reliability that leads the industry.
- Improving customer retention by 10 percent within two years.

WPI.com executives agreed with METASeS and META Group findings that market share in the telecommunications market is highly correlated with customer perceptions of near-transparent network functionality (e.g., reliability, ease of use, etc.), competitive rates, and customer service. WPI.com executives stated that any network disruptions that persisted for more than a very short time (i.e., 15 minutes) were unacceptable to the WPI.com customer base.

Specific information security concerns are:

- Web site vandalism
- Unauthorized access to confidential information
- Denial of Service attacks
- Downstream liability resulting from "pass through" attacks
- Meeting FCC and other regulatory requirements

WPI.com managers were unanimous in their opinion that the company generally is receptive to investing in information security solutions, as long as those solutions are traceable to WPI.com business objectives. WPI.com currently invests approximately 6 percent of its IT budget in information security. This is comparable to the industry standard. In addition to overall budget constraints, WPI.com managers stated that an additional consideration is that the current information security staff is unable to attend more than approximately 40 hours per year of information security training due to the operational tempo maintained within the company. This constraint must be factored into the security solution development process.

As noted in the Key Findings, the assessed information security program at WPI.com is below industry norms as determined by METASeS. While WPI.com's information security posture for the Technology area is consistent with industry norms, WPI.com falls below norms in the Policy Framework, Organization, and Process areas. Figure A-3 summarized the key factors that contributed to the METASeS assessments in these areas. Additional details are provided in Section 3 of this report.

Executive Recommendations

METASeS recommends that WPI.com address the factors (Ref: Figure A-3) that contributed to an overall information security posture that is below industry norms. These factors should be addressed in accordance with a Security Program Development Roadmap (Ref: Section 4) that specifically addresses the Policy Framework, Organization, Technology, and Process areas.

Specifically, METASeS recommends that WPI.com:

- Complete an overall policy, standards, and procedures framework to define the documentation necessary to fully support WPI.com risk management objectives. METASeS further recommends that WPI.com develop specific priorities for developing (or completing) any missing elements of this framework. WPI.com should focus initially on creating an acceptable use policy in the internet and email arenas, as well as technical configuration standards for the critical network (routers, switches) and system platforms (UNIX, Windows NT).

- Appoint a CISO as the single point of ownership for information security.

- Develop a high level information security Concept of Operations (CONOP) that will help WPI.com identify and establish the various organizational interfaces required to maintain the security program. WPI.com will need to assign specific interface owners for each area over time, but should initially focus on interfaces with key business units, core communications operations, IT change management, and the web development organizations.

- Place key servers on protected subnets (e.g., behind screening routers, firewalls, an authentication server, etc.) to implement internal information security measures consistent with industry norms.

- Establish a formal configuration management program to establish and maintain standard system and network configurations. These configurations should support WPI.com business operations while removing unnecessary or unauthorized services and privileges.

- Complete the intrusion detection system deployment and establish a formal incident response capability.

- Implement a formal information security training program for the security staff as well as system and network administrators. This program should be supplemented with basic information security awareness training for the broader WPI.com employee and contractor base.

- Develop and implement a formal risk assessment methodology.

- Establish and maintain a formal security architecture review process that evaluates the current architecture and addresses future changes or additions.

These recommendations and the supporting information security analysis are described in more detail in Section 3 of this report. Section 4 then presents a high-level Risk Mitigation Roadmap for integrating these recommendations into an overall plan for bringing the WPI.com information security posture up to industry norms.

The Risk Mitigation Roadmap presents some immediate (Quick Hit) actions that will allow WPI.com to achieve early, "incremental wins" as the security program is further developed. Such successes are necessary to establish and maintain momentum throughout the organization as the longer term plan is executed. The Roadmap also includes follow-on recommendations for achieving a security posture consistent with METASeS best practices.

NOTE: This location marks the end of the excerpt. In an actual Gap Analysis report, additional text would follow.

Appendix B:
Excerpts from Technology Standards and Configuration Guides Publications

This appendix contains illustrative excerpts and tables of contents from two METASeS best practices publications: *UNIX Security Standards* and the *Solaris 2.6 Server Security Configuration Guide*.

About Technology Standards and Configuration Guides

METASeS Technical Publications are written specifically to address the on-going demands of managing and maintaining your organization's information security program. These publications include:

Technical Standards that provide detailed "rules" defining what should be done at a technology level to mitigate security risks. The standards are related to network or systems infrastructure. For example, a router, an operating system, a switch, or server. Other technical standards are related to business applications (e.g., SAP™, PeopleSoft™, etc.) User-oriented technical standards cover issues like how a user's desktop configuration should be set and maintained or issues like acceptable use of technology resources. For example, mail usage and restrictions, or appropriate Internet surfing, as well as rules for contractors or consultants.

Configuration Guides which provide step-by-step instructions on *how to* set up a piece of equipment, configure an operating system or service, or a security software tool, such that it adheres to the rules detailed in the Technical Standard. For example, our *Solaris 2.6 Server Security Configuration Guide* (SES-ESCFG-OS-SOLSR-26-1.0P) provides step-by-step instructions on how to configure Solaris 2.6 to comply with the *UNIX Security Standards*.

Recommended Reader Background

To comprehend and properly implement the requirements described in this publication, the reader should have an adequate level of understanding of UNIX operating systems, networking protocols (e.g., TCP/IP, FTP, http, smtp), and basic security concepts (e.g., authentication, permissions or exploits).

Symbols and Naming Conventions

The symbols that follow are defined in order to emphasize the METASeS best practices. The use of the RQ (REQUIREMENT) symbol indicates that the information following the symbol defines a requirement related to a Web server security control. The RQ symbol is followed by a number (e.g. RQ-5) to distinguish it from other requirements in the publication and provide an efficient method to reference and locate specific requirements across METASeS publications. Based on research conducted by METASeS, this numbering method helps organizational personnel to reference specific requirements during implementation or auditing of the respective technology. In addition to the requirements (RQs), suggested requirements (SRQs) are also defined throughout the publication. The suggested requirements are presented as an alternative for environments that have a need for a higher level of security controls. They are not considered to be independent requirements but rather a stricter version of the existing requirements (RQs). Lastly, external requirements (ERQs) refer to requirements defined in another document.

RQ #: Requirement followed by the number (replaced with the pound sign #) as it is listed in this publication.

SRQ #: Suggested requirement that is optional for implementation. Its intent is to provide an additional step to increase the security if the system is defined by an RQ.

ERQ #: External requirement that is defined in another publication. In such a reference, additional information is provided.

UNIX Security Standards

Table of Contents

1. Introduction

2. Security Review of UNIX

3. Appendices

Chapter 2: Security Review of UNIX

Account Management

Account Management is an essential component of your Information Security program. As such, your organization must impose standards and guidelines and measurements that protect your organization's valuable assets against intrusion, malicious activity, and unauthorized use. Account management requires the distinction of entities that attain use of system resources for accounting and monitoring purposes. This distinction is provided through identification.

The identification process provides the means to recognize an entity such as system process or a user depending on the credentials presented. Typically, operating systems identify such entities through a pre-defined naming convention (for example, a user-id that distinguishes the entity representation.)

Password security is essential for any multi-user operating system. The strength of every account's password may determine if a system can be compromised during an attack. There are several techniques that an interloper can use to obtain a password on a target system. Just some of the techniques include password cracking, on-line brute force attempts and network traffic monitoring.

The authentication process provides the ability to verify and grant session access to resources maintained by an operating system, provided the authenticated entity (e.g., user or process) has the privileges to perform certain tasks on the system resources. The UNIX operating system provides the mechanism (remote or local) for authenticating users or processes based on the presented credentials provided by the authenticated entity. The credentials may consist of user-id and password or some external authentication mechanisms such as biometrics, tokens, etc. This publication focuses on security features available by UNIX; thus, external authentication mechanisms are not discussed.

Every person who accesses a UNIX computer should have an account. An account is identified by a username and a password. This account information is stored in a file on UNIX systems called /etc/passwd.

The following table identifies some of the primary concerns associated with identification and unauthorized access:

Control Concern	Risk
Users are not uniquely identifiable and accountable.	• If users cannot be uniquely identified, they cannot be held accountable for their actions. • Without user accountability, user control over systems are ineffective.
Weak password controls exist.	• Poor passwords and password controls can compromise system security. • Poor password formation and poor password control could negate user accountability. • Unauthorized users may enter a system more easily.

Control Concern	Risk
Only authorized users can access the system. Authorized users can only perform functions to which they have access.	• Users have unauthorized access to the system. • Users have more access capabilities than they are authorized to have. • User accounts of former employees may still be active when they should not be. • Former employees' user IDs are granted to new employees. Consequently, new employees incorrectly obtain access to files belonging to former employees.
New users are provided access with default settings.	• New users are granted inappropriate access to group membership. • New users are granted inappropriate system access.
Access to a command prompt by users may result in access to utilities, scripts, applications, and data files to which access should not be allowed.	• Information regarding other user's data or applications may be accessible by users that have access to the command prompt. • Shell scripts that are not authorized may be created with undesired consequences by users that have access to the command prompt.
X-Windows can grant session requests based on the IP address of the originator (e.g., using xhost+).	• Unauthorized connections can read the key strokes from the keyboard, capture screens and windows, and execute commands.

Authorization and File Security

Access to all system resources must be on an exception basis only. The concept of permitting the fewest privileges needed to complete a job function must be enforced. Access Control Lists (ACLs) or permissions are used to maintain the permissions and rights that an entity, such as a user or a process, is required to conform to access a requested object.

The following table identifies some of the primary concerns associated with authorization and file security.

Control Concern	Risk
Directories or files with incorrect permissions may allow an attacker to gather sensitive information or gain accesses to the system. For example, if the /etc directory maintains write permissions by everyone, an attacker may insert or remove files (such as /etc/passwd).	File or directory content manipulation by an attacker may lead to a security breach.
Application programs have the ability to change the contents of the application files and directories. Proper permission files or directory manipulation must be maintained by the application, especially if it requires administrative privileges in order to perform some of its functions.	An attacker may manipulate the content of the files that the application is using in order to gain privileged access.

The following requirements are defined to help you establish a set of security guidelines that pertain to UNIX authorization and file security:

RQ-39   All system critical files and directories (e.g., /etc, /bin, /usr, /sbin, etc.) must be owned by appropriate system accounts and groups.

RQ-40   Critical system directories and files shall not allow write access to non-privileged users.

RQ-41   Critical system files such as /etc/shadow and /var/log/messages shall not allow read access to non-privileged users.

RQ-42   Disk device files must not be readable or writable by non-privileged users.

RQ-43   There must be no device files outside of the /dev directory.

RQ-44   Any files with the set-user-id (SUID) or set-group-id (SGID) bit enabled must be inspected to ensure protection against attacks such as race conditions, symbolic links or environmental variables (e.g., $TERM). The existence of these programs or scripts must be verifiable.

RQ-45   The default umask must be set in the /etc/pro file with a value of 027.

RQ-46   Permissions on Startup files and Home directories must be monitored to ensure write access by the rightful owner.

RQ-47   .exrc files must be eliminated unless required. These files should be owned by the user and deny write access by others.

RQ-48   If jobs are scheduled using the "crontab" or "at" command process with root authority, only those individuals with root access shall be permitted to set up the jobs.

Solaris 2.6 Server Security Configuration Guide

Table of Contents

6. Account Management

7. Authentication

8. File System

9. Managing Services

10. Auditing and Logging

11. Appendices

Chapter 3: Physical Security

Physical Security

Computers are vulnerable to physical attacks as well as hacking. An intruder may walk up to the console of a server and attempt to gain unauthorized access through different techniques such as booting from a floppy or CD-ROM, or subverting the screen saver protection. The environmental and physical conditions of any network element's location play an important role in its overall security. Some of the threats associated with physical security include vandalism, unauthorized access, natural disasters and fraud. Although general guidelines regarding physical security for network elements are documented in a separate METASeS publication, it is useful to provide some insight on this matter. This section addresses some general physical security controls for administering Solaris 2.6 systems.

Chapter 6: Account Management

Account Management

Account management is an essential part of any information security program where an organization must impose standards and guidelines to provide measures against malicious or unauthorized use. The Solaris 2.6 operating system provides several built-in group and user accounts, as described below, that require security controls to discourage malicious attacks associated with built-in accounts, or existing or newly created accounts. Account management requires the specification or distinction of entities that attain use of system resources for accounting and monitoring purposes. This distinction is provided through identification.

The identification process provides the means of recognizing an entity (such as system process) or a user based upon the presented credentials. Typically, operating systems identify such entities through a predefined naming convention, such as a user ID, which provides a distinction of the entity representation. The following sections provide the actions required to alter the default configuration of a Solaris 2.6 server in order to elevate the account security. The parameters and settings indicated are based on the requirements defined in the Identification and Authentication sections of *UNIX Security Standards*.

User Groups

The Solaris 2.6 operating system provides the ability to define user groups in order to segment an organization's user community. The following figure depicts the steps for configuring a group, that is, creating, deleting or modifying it, using the Admintool:

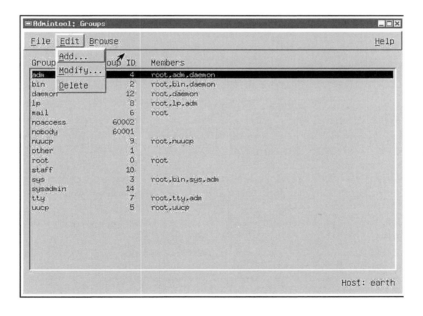

Figure B-1: Using Admintool to Configure User Groups

The steps in modifying a group are:

1. Start Admintool (e.g. #admintool &).

2. Select Browse→Groups.

3. You may highlight the group you wish to modify, delete, or add, through the Edit option.

Default User Accounts

Solaris 2.6 provides the following accounts during the initial installation:
- adm
- bin
- daemon
- listen
- lp
- noaccess
- nobody
- nuucp
- root
- smtp
- sys
- uucp

The following accounts should not be assigned an interactive shell:
- adm
- daemon
- listen
- noaccess
- nobody
- smtp

Assigning non-interactive shells such as /dev/null or /dev/false is one method for protecting these accounts from unauthorized attempts. If any of these accounts are not used, remove them. For example, if the host has been configured only as a Web server, then the smtp account may be removed if the same host will not handle e-mail.

You can remove user accounts: 1) through the command line interface using the userdel command (e.g., $userdel -r smtp); 2) through the Admintool as described below.

You can assign accounts to non-interactive shells through the Admintool or the command line interface by editing the /etc/passwd file. For example:

```
root:x:0:1:Super-User:/:/sbin/sh
daemon:x:1:1::/:
bin:x:2:2::/usr/bin:
sys:x:3:3::/:/dev/null
adm:x:4:4:Admin:/var/adm:
lp:x:71:8:Line Printer Admin:/usr/spool/lp:
smtp:x:0:0:Mail Daemon User:/:
uucp:x:5:5:uucp Admin:/usr/lib/uucp:
nuucp:x:9:9:uucp Admin:/var/spool/uucppublic:/usr/lib/uucp/uucico
listen:x:37:4:Network Admin:/usr/net/nls:
```

```
nobody:x:60001:60001:Nobody:/:
noaccess:x:60002:60002:No Access User:/:
nobody4:x:65534:65534:SunOS 4.x Nobody:/:
```

The accounts `daemon`, `bin`, `adm`, and `lp` are not assigned a shell. In addition, the account sys is assigned a non-interactive shell.

NOTE-RQ-26   Assigning non-interactive shells to default (or not used) accounts fulfills RQ-26 as described in *UNIX Security Standards*.

In addition, you may set additional password configuration settings, as follows:

1. Edit the file `/etc/default/passwd`.

PASSLENGTH is the minimal acceptable password length. Consider setting this to at least 6 characters.

NOTE-RQ-9 This action would address RQ-9 in *UNIX Security Standards*.

MINWEEKS and MAXWEEKS can be used to set a password aging scheme. MINWEEKS is the minimum amount of weeks required before a password change is allowed. MAXWEEKS is the maximum amount of weeks a password is valid until it has to be changed.

NOTE-RQ-10   Setting these parameters would address RQ-10 in *UNIX Security Standards*.

2. Edit the file `/etc/default/login`.

3. Make sure the entry `PASSREQ=YES` exists and is not commented out. This means a password is required for login.

NOTE-RQ-5 This addresses RQ-5 in *UNIX Security Standards*.

Non-Privileged Accounts

This section provides procedures for adding, deleting or configuring user account information. It should be noted that non-privileged users should not be configured to have a UID of 0 (zero) since this is reserved to indicate superuser or system mode. Instead, a high-numbered UID such as 500 can be assigned. Typically, user accounts receive sequentially numbered and high-numbered ID's, e.g., 5000 to 5999, depending on the size of the organization. Maintenance of user accounts can be performed through the Admintool shown in the figure on the following page.

The steps in modifying non-privileged accounts are:

1. Start Admintool (e.g. #admintool &).

2. Select BrowsefiUsers.

3. Select the Edit option to add , modify, or delete the user account settings.

Unused built-in accounts can be deleted or renamed using the Admintool or the command line interface and by editing the `/etc/passwd` file.

NOTE-RQ-24   This task fulfills requirement RQ-24 described in *UNIX Security Standards*.

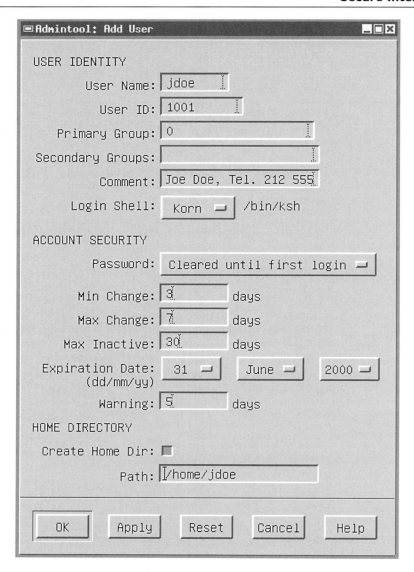

Figure B-2: Adding a User Through Admintool

Administrative Accounts

Administrative accounts that maintain a user ID of 0 (zero) cannot be configured through the Admintool in Solaris 2.6. Instead, configure them through the command line interface using an editor or through the `userdel` and `useradd` commands to delete and add a user. The UID for administrative accounts may be 0 (zero), 1 (one) or some other low-numbered ID to distinguish administrative rights. It should be noted that the UID 0 (zero) should be assigned with extreme care to accounts because it provides system status to the assigned user.

To reconfigure the administrative account, change root's `ROOTDIR` from `/` to `/root`. This changes:

```
root:x:0:1:Super-User:/:/sbin/sh
to: root:x:0:1:Super-User:/root:/sbin/sh
```

Then make sure `/root` is a directory that exists, as follows:

```
# mkdir /root
# chown root /root
# chmod 700 /root
```

Account Directories

Typically, user directories are created on a separate file system to protect the user files from file system corruption. Corruption can occur if the files coexist within another file system that maintains system or application software. The default permissions that should be assigned upon creation of a user directory should be rwx (read, write and execute) for the owner only. For administrative accounts, maintain a separate directory (e.g., `/users/adm`) that holds all the administrator's directories. The following table provides an example of the permissions that should be maintained for user accounts.

Directory	Permissions	Comment
/users/	rwxr-x--x	Maintain read, write and execute permissions for the owner, read and execute permissions for users that belong in the same group, and execute permission for the world.
/users/adm	rwx-r-x---	Maintain read, write and execute permissions for the owner, and read and execute permission for users that belong in the same group.
/users/eng	rwx-r-x--x	Maintain read, write and execute permissions for the owner, read and execute permissions for users that belong in the same group, and execute permission for the world.
/users/eng /joe	rwx------	Maintain read, write and execute permissions for the owner only. If the owner wishes to share files or directories, she can do so by defining explicitly what files and directories should be shared.

To provide the ability to create files or directories in read, write or execute mode by the owner only, the umask value must be set in two files.

The first file is `/etc/profile`, where the global (and root's) umask is defined. The profile file should contain a line with the value 027 or 077 (umask 027). The 027 value provides the ability to create files or directories that have read, write and execute permissions for the user, read and execute permissions for the group, and no permissions for the world. The 077 value restricts read, write and execute permissions to the user only. The same command and value also should be contained in the user's profile. The second file is the `skel` file. Typically, Solaris provides a default directory `/etc/skel` that contains a skeleton profile. The information in that directory is used when a new account is created and thereafter.

NOTE-RQ-45   Setting the umask value to 027 (or 077) fulfills RQ-45 in *UNIX Security Standards*.

User Profile

The user profile defines environment variables, such as default paths or terminal modes that are used to set up the environment for a user upon logon. Typically, a global profile exists in the `/etc directory` that defines global variables for every user. Each user can create and maintain her own profile, but it will be executed after the global profile is executed. The following procedures help configure environmental variables in the `/etc/profile`:

Control	Profile Setting
Grant read, write and execute permissions to the owner upon initial creation of the file or directory .	`umask 077`
Search path should include system directories first and owner directories second.	Configure the path to contain the . (dot), which indicates the current directory to be set at the end of the PATH so that other directories take precedence. E.g.: `$PATH=/usr/bin:/usr/openwin /bin:.`
Display the user quota.	`quota -v username`
Display last login.	The `last` command can be used in the startup scripts to indicate the user's last login. For example, `last n 1 username`. Although this is included in the default installation of Solaris 2.6, you should verify this setting and perform any necessary changes.
Allow the user to break through the execution of the profile during the message of the day only.	Trap `"trap `'2" 2 /bin/cat -s /etc/motd trap "" 2`

Appendix C:
Resources for Information Security & Policy

This appendix contains links to relevant sites on Information Security.

Web Sites

Center for Education and Research in Information Assurance and Security (CERIAS)

http://www.cerias.purdue.edu/

CERIAS is the world's foremost university center for multidisciplinary research and education in areas of Information Security (computer security, network security, and communications security) and information assurance. This site provides an extensive hot list of security links, as well as a huge archive of freeware security tools.

NIST Computer Security Resource Clearinghouse

http://csrc.nist.gov/

The National Institutes for Standards Technologies Web site. Provides pointers to relevant Federal regulations, such as Computer Security Act of 1987 and Circular A-130, as well as several sample policy documents. Some of their papers are available, plus links to other sites. One of its interesting links to policy-related materials is:

http://csrc.nist.gov/policies/welcome.html

The Computer Crime and Intellectual Property Section

http://www.cybercrime.gov/

Issues and pointers for computer crime and policy from the Criminal Division of the United States Department of Justice.

United States Government Electronic Commerce Policy

http://www.ecommerce.gov/

A resource site for United States and international news, white papers, and policy on global electronic commerce.

The Electronic Frontier Foundation (EFF)

http://www.eff.org/

The EFF was founded in 1990 to ensure that essential civil liberties are protected as new communication technologies emerge.

Electronic Privacy Information Center (EPIC)

http://www.epic.org/

A public interest group in Washington D.C., established in 1994 to focus public attention on emerging civil liberties issues and to protect privacy. Also has information on encryption controls. See the Policy Archives on Computer Security and Privacy for relevant articles.

Foundation for Information Policy Research (FIPR)

www.fipr.org

FIPR has information on UK and European Union encryption controls.

Windows IT Security

http://www.ntsecurity.net/

A good site for security information and tools for Microsoft products.

People for Internet Responsibility

http://www.pfir.org/

Founded by two well-known privacy advocates and policy experts, Peter Neumann and Lauren Weinstein, PFIR is a resource for discussion, analysis, and information regarding Internet issues.

SecurityFocus

http://www.securityfocus.com/

SecurityFocus.com is a computer security Web portal designed to spark discussion on security-related topics, create security awareness, and provide the Internet's largest and most comprehensive database of security knowledge and resource. This site provides access to security links and resources, including news, books, mailing lists, tools and products, and security services.

Software Publishers Association (SPA) Anti-Piracy Web Page

http://www.siia.net/piracy/

An interesting set of pointers, including guidelines for copyright protection, Internet usage policies, and anti-piracy information.

References

NIST Special Publication 800-XX Internet Security Policy: A Technical Guide

http://csrc.nist.gov/isptg/html

Developed to provide organizations with guidance on how to create a coherent Internet-specific information security policy. Addresses the most critical current topics and provides sample policy statements for low-, medium-, and high-risk environments.

Site Security Handbook -- RFC 1244 July 1991

http://www.faqs.org/rfcs/rfc1244.html

The original version of the Site Security Handbook. While this version has been replaced by RFC 2196 and much of its information is dated, it still contains some useful discussion related to policy issues.

Site Security Handbook -- RFC 2196 September 1997

http://www.faqs.org/rfcs/rfc2196.html

Very useful guide to developing computer security policies and procedures for sites that have systems on the Internet. Subjects covered include policy content and format, technical discussions of the more common vulnerabilities faced today, suggested policy countermeasures, and incident response planning. An excellent list of references is also included.

Safeguarding Your Technology: Practical Guidelines for Electronic Education Information Security

http://nces.ed.gov/pubsearch/pubsinfo.asp?pubid=98297

A well-organized handbook developed by the National Center for Education Statistics and discussing a variety of security issues.

A Guide to Developing Computing Policy Documents

http://www.usenix.org/sage/publications/policies

Part of the System Administration Guild (SAGE) series of publications entitled Short Topics in System Administration. The booklet provides justifications for why a site needs policies and suggests what a policy document should contain. Contains a useful template for a computing policy document.

System Security: A Management Perspective

`http://www.usenix.org/sage/publications/syssec.html`

Another booklet in the SAGE series, this publication discusses many of the activities that are required to support a security policy development effort such as security planning, identifying threats and assets, and evaluating effectiveness of safeguards.

Books

Building an Information Security Awareness Program
Author: Mark B. Desman
Publisher: Auerbach Publications
Copyright Date: 2002
ISBN: 0-8493-0116-5

Computer Crime: A Crimefighter's Handbook
Authors: David Icove, Karl Seger and William Von Storch
Publisher: O'Reilly & Associates, Inc.
Copyright Date: 1995
ISBN: 1-56592-086-4

Computer Security Basics
Authors: Deborah Russell & G.T. Gangemi, Sr.
Publisher: O'Reilly & Associates, Inc.
Copyright Date: 1991
ISBN: 0-937175-71-4

Corporate Espionage
Author: Ira Winkler
Publisher: Prima
Copyright Date: 1997
ISBN: 0-7615-0840-6

E-Policy: How to Develop Computer, E-mail, and Internet Guidelines to Protect Your Company and Its Assets
Author: Michael Overly
Publisher: AMACOM Books
Copyright Date: 1998
ISBN: 0-8144-7996-0

Fighting Computer Crime
Author: Donn Parker
Publisher: John Wiley & Sons
Copyright Date: 1998
ISBN: 0471163783

The Hacker's Handbook: A Guide for Information Security, Network, and System Administrators
Authors: John D. Tessel, Susan Young, and Felix Lindner
Publisher: Auerbach Publications
Copyright Date: 2002
ISBN: 0-8493-0888-7

Information Security Architecture: An Integrated Approach to Security in the Organization
Author: Jan Killmeyer Tudor
Publisher: Auerbach Publications
Copyright Date: 2001
ISBN: 0-8493-9988-2

Information Security Policies
Author: Charles Cresson Woods
Publisher: Baseline Software
Copyright Date: 1999
ISBN 1-881585-06-9

Information Security Policies and Procedures: A Practioner's Reference
Author: Thomas Peltier
Publisher: Auerbach Publications
Copyright Date: 1999
ISBN: 1-8493-9996-3

Information Security Policies, Procedures, and Standards: Guidelines for Effective Information Security Management
Author: Thomas Peltier
Publisher: Auerbach Publications
Copyright Date: 2002
ISBN: 0-8493-1137-3

Information Security Risk Analysis
Author: Thomas Peltier
Publisher: Auerbach Publications
Copyright Date: 2001
ISBN: 1-8493-0880-1

Mastering Network Security
Author: Chris Brenton
ISBN: 0-7821-2343-0

The NCSA Guide to Disaster Recovery Planning
Author: Miora
ISBN: 0-07-042904-9

Practical Guide to Security Engineering and Information Assurance
Author: Debra S. Herrman
Publisher: Auerbach Publications
Copyright Date: 2002
ISBN: 1-8493-1163-2

Practical UNIX and Internet Security, 2nd Edition
Author: Simson Garfinkel and Gene Spafford
Publisher: O'Reilly & Associates, Inc.
Copyright Date: 1996
ISBN: 1-56592-148-8

Secure Computing: Threats and Safeguards
Author: Rita Summers
Publisher: McGraw-Hill
Copyright Date: 1997
ISBN: 0-07-069419-2

Securing E-Business Applications and Communications
Authors: Jonathan S. Held and John Bowers
Publisher: Auerbach Publications
Copyright Date: 2001
ISBN: 1-8493-0963-8

The Security of Network Architectures: Design and Assessment
Authors: Jody Fraser and Jonathan Hackmann
Publisher: Auerbach Publications
Copyright Date: 2002
ISBN: 1-8493-1249-3

Appendix D:
Examples of Processes and Procedures

This appendix provides examples of processes and procedures, as follows:

- Core Security Processes
- Information Security Procedures
- Information Technology Processes
- Business Processes

Core Security Processes

Core security processes are typically owned (created and refined) and performed by the security organization, or a matrix team with security responsibility.

Process	Definition
Security Program Management	The ongoing management, review and refinement of the elements of the Information Security program, including policies, standards, procedures, processes, technology, and organization. Addresses changing risk and business conditions.
Risk Management	The ongoing, methodical assessment of Information Security risks across the organization.
Policy Management	An ongoing (life cycle) process for defining and refining the organization's Information Security policy framework elements (policy, procedures, standards).
Threat Management	The ongoing monitoring (e.g., open source data collection) and management (deterrence, mitigation, tracking, etc.) of Information Security- related threats. Treats are would-be perpetrators (people/organizations) of Information Security breaches.
Vulnerability Management	The ongoing monitoring and management of Information Security vulnerabilities. Vulnerabilities are the holes that threats could exploit to breach Information Security.
Security Administration	Adding, changing user, group, or system privileges.

Process	Definition
Security Architecture	Development and ongoing maintenance of the security architecture -- typically a subarchitecture or domain of the enterprise-wide technical architecture. This process may also refer to the development and maintenance of a portfolio of system-level architecture/design templates enabling rapid deployment of new systems through the use of baseline best practice templates.
Information Security Training & Awareness	Development and ongoing maintenance of the security education program. This includes awareness activities oriented towards the end users (employees, customers, partners, etc.), as well as training on Information Security policy, processes, architectures, procedures, etc. for the IT organization (e.g., applications development, operations).

Information Security Procedures

Information Security procedures are typically created and refined by the security organization or a matrix team with security responsibility. Procedures are differentiated from processes by their scope and duration. Procedures are typically of short duration (a few minutes of days), while processes are more often long-running (days, weeks, months) or continuous in nature.

Information Security Procedure	Definition
Technical Configuration Procedures (a.k.a. system hardening procedures).	Specific instructions on how to configure various systems (network & system devices, applications, etc.) such that they comply with the organization's Security Standards. Organizations typically require a portfolio of Technical Configuration Procedures to address the multiple systems in use.
Media Sanitation	The procedure for disposing of information that contains sensitive data.
Vulnerability Assessments (a.k.a. penetration testing, ethical hacking)	The instructions on what and how to test an Information Technology environment and uncover vulnerabilities (both system and non-system level).
Incident Response	Instructions to handle potential or real security breaches. The procedure typically includes an incident prioritization method, escalation instructions and matrix of resources to involve based on the type and severity of the incident.
Incident Investigation/Forensics	The procedures for researching the source of a breach and gathering evidentiary data in support of potential future civil or criminal litigation.
Threat Assessment	The procedures for analyzing specific threats to an organizational asset (or set of assets).
Asset Classification	Instructions/guidance that information/data owners can use to appropriately value and label the information/data in question, such that it receives the appropriately secure treatment (both via technical and non-technical controls). Part of asset classification is system zoning, formal zones that identify infrastructure grouping by priority. Corresponds to the level of monitoring implemented for certain systems.

IT (Information Technology) Processes

IT (Information Technology) processes are typically managed by various IT departments, but require some level of integration with security processes and procedures.

Process Relationship to Information Security	Process Definition
Configuration Management Information Security Relationship -- Vulnerability management process and vulnerability assessment procedures to ensure known problems are fixed (e.g., via patches or service packs) and new problems are not introduced to the environment.	The process for making modifications to systems including: hardware, operating systems, network operating systems, application systems, etc. The configuration management process typically also endeavors to document the physical and logical relationships and specific configuration of system elements.
Change Management Information Security Relationship -- Vulnerability management process to ensure that appropriate security sign-offs are completed so that new vulnerabilities are not introduced to the environment.	The communication, tracking, and approval of modifications to the production environment for new systems or various configuration modifications, such that they are performed in an orderly, controlled manner to minimize adverse impacts and enable rapid recovery in the event of a problem. Broad categories of change may affect certain systems, e.g., programmatic changes, system updates (patches), configuration changes (OS or middleware). Each change may activate high-level responses. System updates may require that a system be recertified within certain days of the change. Significant changes to middleware (WWW server) applications require manual examination by Information Security.
Contingency Planning/Disaster Recovery Information Security Relationship -- Ongoing threat management process and security incident response procedures to ensure the cross communication and orderly restoration of systems in the event of a security breach. Also the risk assessment process so that the proposed contingency/disaster recover plan does not introduce security vulnerabilities (e.g., offsite storage of sensitive backup media may require additional controls).	Process designed to minimize the impact of adverse events and ensure an orderly restoration of the IT capability supporting the business. The adverse events can derive from either man-made and natural disasters, and may stem from accidental or purposeful acts. They include natural disasters, or intentional acts like sabotage or security breaches (e.g., Denial of Service attacks).
Enterprise-Wide IT Architecture Information Security Relationship -- Security architecture is a subarchitecture (or component architecture) of the enterprise-wide IT architecture.	An enterprise-wide technical architecture (EWTA) is a logically consistent set of principles that guides the "engineering" -- that is, detailed design, selection, construction, implementation, deployment, support, and management of an organization's information systems and technology infrastructure. Consequently, a set of product standards, by itself, does not constitute architecture. What is most important is guidance on how the products are to be used to achieve the enterprise's goals.
Systems Development Life Cycle (SDLC) Information Security Relationship -- Security architecture, risk assessment, vulnerability assessments, security administration. The SDLC needs to incorporate various security tasks so that appropriate security is built into the systems rather than bolted on afterwards.	The process that governs how systems are built, or modified to meet the organization's needs. This includes COTS (commercial off the shelf) systems that can be purchased and deployed or purchased and modified/integrated to fulfill requirements.

Process Relationship to Information Security	Process Definition
IT operations (a.k.a. data center operations or network operations (NOC)) Information Security Relationship -- Threat management, incident response. The NOC or data center operations staff often provides off-hours threat event monitoring and initial incident response triage steps.	The ongoing monitoring of systems to ensure that potential problems are recognized and fixed prior to when problems or outages would be identified and addressed within defined service-level targets.
Help Desk/Problem Management Information Security Relationship -- Threat management, incident response, security administration (e.g., for password resets).	The process for tracking customer calls and service outages such that issues are resolved within service level parameters.

Business Processes

Business processes are maintained outside of the IT department, and require integration with various Information Security processes or procedures.

Process Relationship to Information Security	Process Definition
Employee Life Cycle Information Security Relationship -- Security administration (add, change, or remove system privileges).	The HR processes/procedures dealing with the hiring, training, promotion/demotion, or removal of employees.
Merger & Acquisition (M&A) and Divestiture Information Security Relationship -- Risk management, risk assessment (as part of due diligence), security administration, security architecture.	The business process for assessing (due diligence) and then executing mergers/acquisitions, or divestitures.
Regulatory Compliance Management Information Security Relationship -- Risk assessment	The process for maintaining compliance with regulations and laws administered by such agencies as HIPPA and the SEC. While the legal department of an organization has responsibility for this matter, Information Security must be aware of areas that impact it. In banking, for example, regulatory boards can impose fines or sanctions for technical non-compliance.
Customer Processes Information Security Relationship -- Security administration	Processes designed to add, delete, or change customers.
Partner Processes Information Security Relationship -- Security administration, security architecture (for system-level integration), vulnerability assessment	Processes designed for adding, deleting, or changing partners (suppliers, distributors, resellers, etc.)
Audit Information Security Relationship -- Risk management, risk assessment, security administration	Process for review of financial and other official business operations.
Public Relations Information Security Relationship -- Incident response (for "spin control" of breaches).	Process for orderly dissemination of information relating to the organization
Product Development Information Security Relationship -- Risk assessment, security architecture (where new products contain an IT component)	The process for creating new hard goods or service products for sale.

Process Relationship to Information Security	Process Definition
Certification Information Security Relationship -- Risk management, risk assessment, security administration, vulnerability assessment	A formal process of signing off on the functionality and security of new systems.
Physical Security Information Security Relationship -- Physical access controls to IT infrastructure and systems	The process (or organization) responsible for securing the physical assets of the organization.

Appendix E:
Trends in Security Spending

This appendix contains excerpts from the May 1999 report, *Enterprise Security in Practice: Market Segments in Transition*, by META Group. The report was based on a survey of how organizations allocate their security expenditures.

The excerpts contain a number of data tables, whose terminology bears some explanation for those unaccustomed to statistical analysis.

In the tables, the "Frequency" column denotes the number of respondents, who totaled 529. The "Percent" column breaks down the responses by percentage. The "Valid Percent" column also breaks down responses by percentage, while leaving out "invalid" responses where, for example, a question did not apply to a respondent or where a respondent did not answer the question.

Some tables also contain mean and median values. The mean is the average value of a set of numbers. The median is the middle value in a set of values arranged in order of size. Further, the term "Count" refers to the tally of respondents.

Excerpts from Enterprise Security in Practice, Market Segments in Transition

....In recent years, as IT organizations have grown and become an integral part of the business organizations that depend on and feed IT for its own information needs, security needs have grown in parallel. This section will describe the current IT environment, with an emphasis on the security organizations and infrastructure now in place.

The makeup of the survey was:

- From 50 to 1,000 employees constitute 30.4% of the sample (n = 161)
- From 1,000 to 5,000 employees constitute 28.2% of the sample (n = 149)
- More than 5,000 employees constitute 41.4% of the sample (n = 219)

As the survey was implemented, it became apparent that identifying individuals with security responsibilities was going to be a more challenging task than previously thought. Calls were made to more than 10,000 organizations and, for various reasons, resulted in the 529 completed surveys this research is based on. Several other restrictions were placed on the interviewing process as well. Only a maximum of 10% of the sample could be without information security or plans to invest in information security. However, only 7% of the sample fell into that category, so the quota was never even approached, let alone breached. Finally, a ceiling of no more than 15% of the sample was placed on government and educational organizations.

Figures E-1 and E-2 set the larger stage of the overall IT organization. As can be seen, there is a broad spread of IT expenditures represented by these organizations. Just under 30% of those knowledgeable of their IT budget have less than $500,000, while 12% have annual IT budgets above $100 million.

	Frequency	Percent	Valid Percent
Over $100M	49	9.3	12.0
$20M-$100M	55	10.4	13.4
$3M-$20M	109	20.6	26.7
$500K-$3M	75	14.2	18.3
Under 500K	121	22.9	29.6
Total	409	77.3	100.0
System Missing	120	22.7	
Total	120	22.7	
Total	529	100.0	

Figure E-1: Present IT Budget — Organization

	Frequency	Percent	Valid Percent
Manufacturing	132	25.0	25.0
Finance/Banking/Insurance/Real Estate	123	23.3	23.3
Business/Professional Services	62	11.7	11.7
Transportation/Communications/Utilities	52	9.8	9.8
Wholesale/Retail Trade	487	9.1	9.1
Public Administration/Government	42	7.9	7.9
Healthcare	37	7.0	7.0
Education	19	3.6	3.6
Agriculture/Mining/Construction	12	2.3	2.3
Other	2	.4	.4
Total	529	100.0	100.0
Total	529	100.0	

Figure E-2: What is the Primary Business or Industry of Your Company

Figure E-2 reviews the industrial classification of the respondents. Manufacturing is most heavily represented, followed by FIRE (an amalgam of financial services industries, including finance/banking, insurance, and real estate). Together, they compose 48% of the sample.

Figure E-3 represents the range of security budgets. Again, there is a broad spread with 16.7% of the organizations having less than $5,000 and 22.7% having more than $500,000. Of the latter group, there are nine very large organizations with over $10,000,000 in annual information security expenditures. The under $5,000 category includes 11% (n = 40) of the sample, which had no security expenditures at all.

	Frequency	Percent	Valid Percent
Over $500K	83	15.7	22.7
$100K-$500K	82	15.5	22.5
$20K-$100K	100	18.9	27.4
$5K-$20K	39	7.4	10.7
Under $5,000	61	11.5	16.7
Total	365	69.0	100.0
System Missing	164	31.0	
Total	164	31.0	
Total	529	100.0	

Figure E-3: How Large is Your Security Budget

However, we warn that incorrect conclusions could be drawn from the data in Figure E-3 and note that there is a very large correlation between security budgets and many proxies of organization size. Strong relationships exist between the size of the security budget and the following:

- IT budget (Pearson's correlation = 0.878 significant at 0.001 level)
- Number of total employees (Pearson's correlation = 0.466 significant at 0.001 level)
- Number of IT employees (Pearson's correlation = 0.271 significant at 0.001 level)
- Number of IT clients (Pearson's correlation = 0.216 significant at 0.001 level)

Because this is the case, trying to draw conclusions regarding the intensity of investment in security, and any of the other factors we are about to analyze, will actually be measuring the size of the organization as well (sometimes called "co-linearity"). To compensate for this, Figure E-4 uses a per-capita security budget figure. This is a far superior measure as to how dedicated a given organization is to investing in information security.

As can be seen, 12.9% of the knowledgeable sample have zero expenditures, while 11.5% spend more than $400 per employee.

Information security is still in its infancy, and as such, investments are likely to grow rapidly. In fact, these organizations plan to spend a mean of $2.8 million during the next 12 months versus the $2.3 million they averaged in the current year. That is a growth figure of approximately 22%. The median figures are $115,000 for the next 12 months and $100,000 for the current year, a growth rate of 15%. The reason for the distinction between the two figures is that the larger organizations will be growing faster. In fact, a separate analysis demonstrates that those organizations with current security budgets over $100,000 will be growing at a 50% rate during the next year.

Figure E-5 examines the distribution of security budgets forecasted in 12 months. Comparing this figure to Figure E-3, we find that, of those knowledgeable, the percent of enterprises with security budgets under $5,000 declines from 22.7% to 16% of the sample. Conversely, the highest spenders, those with more than a $500,000 budget, increase in share from 16.7% to 28.8%. Clearly, security is on the early slope of their growth curve.

	Frequency	Percent	Valid Percent
No Budget	47	8.9	12.9
$1-$10 per employee	42	7.9	11.5
$11-$50 per employee	108	20.4	29.6
$50-$200 per employee	91	17.2	24.9
$200-$400 per employee	35	6.6	9.6
Over $400 per employee	42	7.9	11.5
Total	365	69.0	100.0
System Missing	164	31.0	
Total	164	31.0	
Total	529	100.0	

Figure E-4: Per Capita Security Budget

	Frequency	Percent	Valid Percent
Under 5K	56	10.6	16.0
$5K-$20K	32	6.0	9.1
$20K-$100K	78	14.7	22.2
$100K-$500K	84	15.9	23.9
Over $500K	101	19.1	28.8
Total	351	66.4	100.0
System Missing	178	33.6	
Total	178	33.6	
Total	529	100.0	

Figure E-5: Estimated Security Budget in 12 Months

Figures E-6 and E-7 analyze security and per-capita expenditures by industry. Figure E-6 demonstrates that two industries, manufacturing and FIRE, are much more heavily weighted toward security spending than the balance of the industries, due to organization size and actual expenditure levels.

Figure E-7 examines the per-capita equivalent. In this examination, it can be seen that manufacturing still leads in security expenditures. While the government sector has emerged as the second most important under the mean, it shows up as second to last in median expenditures. Translated, there is a large variance in security spending among government-sector organizations. In contrast, FIRE expenditures are third highest under the mean and highest under the median. This segment is the highest security spender in general, even though it is influenced by a small number of very large organizations.

	Median	Count
Manufacturing	$4,311,745	132
Finance/Banking/Insurance/Real Estate	$3,306,759	123
Business/Professional Services	$1,346,711	52
Transportation/Communications/Utilities	$1,144,789	62
Wholesale/Retail Trade	$677,819	48
Public Administration/Government	$267,773	37
Healthcare	$192,630	42
Education	$176,000	19
Agriculture/Mining/Construction	$100,000	12
Other		2

Figure E-6: Mean Security Budget by Industry

	Mean	Median	Count
Manufacturing	$552	$36	132
Finance/Banking/Insurance/Real Estate	$486	$31	123
Business/Professional Services	$339	$100	52
Transportation/Communications/Utilities	$213	$68	62
Wholesale/Retail Trade	$145	$50	48
Public Administration/Government	$115	$39	37
Healthcare	$111	$34	42
Education	$87	$33	19
Agriculture/Mining/Construction	$12	$11	12
Other			2
	$320	$50	529

Figure E-7: Per Capita Security Budget by Industry

.... [There] are a relatively small number of key factors that distinguish organizations from each other in their attitudes and purchasing behavior concerning security products and services. This section will highlight two major segments that best define security market segments:

- Size of organization
- Third-party access to the organization's networks, which we will refer to here as the "amalgam"

Figure E-8[2] shows the per-capita security budget, broken down by company size and installed networks. Respondents were segmented into "classes" based on number of employees, with classes described as very large (>5,000 employees), large (1,000-4,999 employees), medium (500-999 employees), and small (50-499 employees). The average per-capita security budget is shown for respondents with and without specific installed networks (LAN, WAN, Internet, VPN, extranet, intranet).

[1] The data is being compared to another META Group study that used a similar stratified sample, biased to larger companies.

[2] Please note, where the "No" line is missing, there were too few respondents in that cell, and the data was statistically insignificant and volatile. This is primarily a result of the high penetration rates for several of the network types.

			Quota Class Size			
Which of the following are present in your organization?			**5000+** (very large) per capita security budget	**1000-4999** (large) per capita security budget	**500-999** (medium) per capita security budget	**50-499** (small) per capita security budget
LAN	Yes	Mean	$264	$431	$198	$345
		Count	219	149	56	102
WAN	Yes	Mean	$186	$449	$225	$493
		Count	214	141	47	62
	No	Mean		$77	$64	$147
		Count		8	9	43
Internet Access	Yes	Mean	$266	$377	$198	$353
		Count	217	146	55	100
VPN	Yes	Mean	$178	$631	$178	$922
		Count	135	61	27	23
	No	Mean	$409	$264	$220	$211
		Count	84	88	29	82
Extranet	Yes	Mean	$183	$228	$210	$696
		Count	139	61	20	10
	No	Mean	$414	$575	$190	$305
		Count	80	88	36	95
Intranet	Yes	Mean	$276	$486	$205	$432
		Count	209	123	47	68
	No	Mean		$141	$152	$160
		Count		26	9	37

Figure E-8: Installed Networks by Company Size by Per Capita Security Budget

As shown earlier in this report, there is no question that company size measured on any number of attributes impacts both the scale and type of investments in security products. This is the case because of the obvious need to build suitable infrastructure to cover the security needs of a larger number of workers. In addition, larger organizations tend to be more aggressive in electronic commerce and third-party access initiatives. However, when that scale effect is minimized by using per-capita security expenditures as the basis for comparison, as has been done in Figures E-8 andE-9, the true story changes dramatically.

With few exceptions, the small and large classes of companies are those with the greatest per-capita budget. The high results for the small segment can be explained by the base expenditure an organization must make to institute even rudimentary security. In small organizations, this level of expenditure would need to be amortized over a smaller workforce — hence, the high per-capita expenditures. Large organizations are those just beginning to embark on EC and third-party access initiatives, requiring a more robust security infrastructure and investments in new security technology.

When comparing per-capita security budgets against installed network, the types of installed networks should be viewed as a key variable that leads to the amalgam segments, which will be discussed next. For clarification, we have assumed the following definitions for intranet, VPN, and extranet networks:

- **LAN** (local-area network) — Private, internal networks
- **WAN** (wide-area network) — Dedicated, private (e.g., FR, leased lines) networks connecting remote sites
- **Intranets** — Internal IP network segments, hosting Web-enabled applications primarily for corporate employees
- **VPN** — Encrypted communications, leveraging the Internet or other shared IP network for enabling network access to remote employees or branch offices
- **Extranet** — Shared network segments, accessible to third parties via the Internet or other shared IP network

The installation rate of intranets for very large organizations is high, with no statistically reliable sample of organizations in this class that does not have intranets installed. All three of the other organization classes show dramatically higher per-capita expenditures when an intranet is present. Therefore, intranets are an indicator for IT sophistication and broader investments in security.

LAN	Mean	$358
	Count	246
WAN	Mean	$352
	Count	447
Internet Access	Mean	$321
	Count	526
VPN	Mean	$311
	Count	464
Extranet	Mean	$308
	Count	518
Intranet	Mean	$320
	Count	529

Figure E-9: Mean Per Capita Security Expenditures by Installed Networks

Similarly, per-capita expenditures are significantly higher within organizations with a WAN.

However, organizations with VPNs and extranets behave differently. In the case of VPNs, very large organizations without a VPN spend almost three times more on security than those that do have a VPN. We believe that, for large organizations, VPNs are a more cost-effective alternative to dedicated, private connections offered by value-added network (VAN) service providers. When VANs are used, organizations are often forced to implement security infrastructure for each external connection into the network, while VPNs enable a more leverageable infrastructure that helps reduce costs.

In contrast, small organizations spend several times more on per-capita security if they do have a VPN. This increase in security spending is due to a previous lack of external connections into the network. Because smaller organizations typically cannot afford VAN services, a VPN is their first infrastructure built for third-party access, requiring new investments in security technologies with overall costs amortized over a smaller workforce. While Large organizations also showed an increase in security spending with the presence of a VPN, we believe this is due to the vast uptake of third-party access initiatives within that market sector, driving more VPN deployments and enhanced security infrastructure.

Figure E-9 displays the total per-capita security expenditures by installed networks, regardless of organizational size. As can be seen, organizations with VPNs and intranets lead with the highest per-capita security expenditures, while Internet and extranet installations account for the lowest per-capita expenditures. Because basic Internet access (outbound access for Web browsing) is universal across large and small organizations and requires little more than a firewall for security, it is not surprising to see lower security budgets associated with it. However, the lower budgets indicated for the presence of extranet networks contradicts our expectations. Because an extranet links third-party networks over a public or shared IP network, we would expect it to drive a significant increase in security spending. We attribute these conflicting results to a confusion surrounding the definition of "extranet."

Figure E-10 demonstrates that, for the entire sample, organizations providing remote workers, customers, and suppliers with network access have vastly higher security expenditures than those that do not provide such access. The exception is seen with Internet users, which have no impact on expenditures. Because organizations tend to be more conservative when opening resources to Internet users, usually enabling application access only via a demilitarized zone (DMZ), less security infrastructure is required.

		Median	Count
Remote Workers	Yes	$100,000	481
	No	$10,000	46
Customers	Yes	$200,000	228
	No	$55,000	299
Suppliers	Yes	$300,000	159
	No	$60,000	368
Internet Users	Yes	$100,000	254
	No	$100,000	273

Figure E-10: Which Groups Have Access to LAN/WAN by Mean Security Budget (All Organizations)

FiguresE-11 and E-12 isolate the larger and smaller organizations to see if external access drives security spending without the bias of company size. As can be seen, it does. For the larger organizations (those with IT budgets over $3 million), the difference in security expenditures between those providing and not providing access to the three groups narrows in comparison to the entire sample, but it is still considerable. This time, the impact of smaller security budgets is pronounced, as expenditures drop for those who provide access to Internet users. These lower expenditures are really impacted by that subgroup of organizations that only provide third-party access to Internet users and exclude suppliers and customers. In fact, these Internet-only organizations maintain a median security budget of $100,000.

		Count	Median	Percent
Remote Workers	Yes	265	$250,000	95.0
	No	14	$50,000	5.0
Customers	Yes	142	$300,000	50.9
	No	137	$200,000	49.1
Suppliers	Yes	103	$350,000	36.9
	No	176	$200,000	63.1
Internet Users	Yes	145	$200,000	52.0
	No	134	$250,000	48.0

Figure E-11: Which Have Access to Your Organization's LAN/WAN? By Median Security Budget (Organizations With IT Budgets Over $3M)

Finally, the same analysis is displayed in Figure E-12 for organizations with IT budgets under $3 million. As was predicted by the earlier figures, spending is higher for installed networks across the board, including the Internet. As these organizations start to invest or increase very small expenditures in security, they have no savings to show for the conversion to the Internet.

		Count	Median	Percent
Remote Workers	Yes	150	$20,000	84.3
	No	28	$5,000	15.7
Customers	Yes	54	$15,000	30.3
	No	124	$13,750	69.7
Suppliers	Yes	26	$36,000	14.6
	No	152	$12,000	85.4
Internet Users	Yes	84	$20,000	47.2
	No	94	$10,000	52.8

Figure E-12: Which Have Access to Your Organization's LAN/WAN? By Median Security Budget (Organizations With IT Budgets Under $3M)

This brings us to the final segment concept: the amalgamated organization (depicted in Figure E-13). The definitions of these organizations depend on the external relationships they maintain with various groups:

- **Independent** — Only remote workers are allowed network access
- **Customer-supply chain** — Remote workers, customers, or suppliers
- **Remote/Internet** — Remote workers and Internet users
- **Web feeder** — Remote workers, Internet users, and customers
- **Total amalgamated** — Remote workers, customers, suppliers, and Internet users allowed access
- **Archaic** — No remote employees or third-party access

For example, the "independent" grouping is the most common configuration with 31.3% of the 492 respondents included in this sample grouping.[3]

	Frequency	Percent	Valid Percent
Independent	154	29.1	31.3
Total Amalgamated	88	16.6	17.9
Customer Supply Chain	88	16.6	17.9
Remote/Internet	68	12.9	13.8
Web Feeder	65	12.3	13.2
Archaic	29	5.5	5.9
Total	492	93.0	100.0
System Missing	37	7.0	
Total	37	7.0	
Total	529	100.0	

Figure E-13: Amalgamated Organization

The next two groups are tied for second in frequency: "total amalgamated," which means they maintain all external relationships, and "customer supply chain," which includes remote workers, as well as suppliers or customers or both.

Due to the extent of remote workers, all amalgam segments include them, except for the "archaic" grouping, represented by only 5.9% of the organizations. Using the amalgamated definitions, Figure E-14 displays both the existing and planned median per-capita security budgets, and Figure E-15 displays both the existing and planned median total security budgets.

Figure E-14 demonstrates how heavily each organization spends on security within the confines of its size. Figure E-15 tells how large the available expenditures are at each type of amalgamated organization.

---

[3] There were several configurations that had only incidental membership and were thus excluded from the analysis.

Amalgam		Per-Capita Security Budget	New Per-Capita Security Budget
Customer Supply Chain	Count	88	88
	Median	$59	$100
Indepndent	Count	154	154
	Median	$63	$80
Remote/Internet	Count	68	68
	Median	$56	$58
Total Amalgamated	Count	88	88
	Median	$40	$50
Web Feeder	Count	65	65
	Median	$29	$31
Archaic	Count	29	29
	Median	$20	$22

Figure E-14: Organization Type (Amalgam) by Median Per Capita Security Budget

The first noticeable point is that the leaders in one figure are not the same in the other, because organization size comes mainly into play in Figure E-15. For example, "customer supply chain" organizations have the highest median per-capita security expenditure plans at $100, but they come in second to "total amalgamated" organizations in overall average expenditures for the next 12 months ($321,250).

Likewise, total amalgamated organizations only rank fourth in expected per-capita expenditures ($50), but hold a commanding first place for overall expected security expenditures, with a median of $420,000…

Amalgam		Existing Security Budget	Security Budget in Next 12 Months
Total Amalgamated	Count	88	88
	Median	$150,000	$420,000
Customer Supply Chain	Count	88	88
	Median	$250,000	$321,250
Independent	Count	154	154
	Median	$100,000	$110,000
Web Feeder	Count	65	65
	Median	$100,000	$101,000
Remote/Internet	Count	68	68
	Median	$50,000	$60,000
Archaic	Count	29	29
	Median	$10,000	$10,500

Figure E-15: Organization Type (Amalgam) by Total Security Budget

Glossary

Acceptable use policy: Addresses appropriate business use of the organization's assets. This includes items such as appropriately labeling, handling, and protection of corporate data and information. It also includes appropriate use of the organization's network and computing resources so that the information is not unnecessarily exposed.

Architecture and design: Process for planning and assembling the various technical and non-technical elements of a system to meet the security goals. In the system development life cycle, process, architecture and design describe the structure of the system, and define the program modules and procedures as well as the data structures and algorithms.

Asset value: The worth of the data that intruders target.

Asset identification and classification policy: Allows an organization to better leverage future investments in security and risk management efforts by focusing on critical information assets, and by providing a level of security appropriate to the value of the assets.

Asset management policy: Provides the governance for proper handling and safekeeping of assets, as well as change control and configuration management objectives throughout the asset life cycle.

Asset protection policy: Provides the governance necessary to establish specific standards on the appropriate degree of confidentiality, integrity, and availability for your organization's assets.

Auditability: The ability to track user or system activity for future reference or through real-time monitoring and logging.

Authentication server: A network device that challenges network entities, including computers and people, for their credentials to determine that they are who they claim to be.

Authentication: The process or ability to identify a person, resource, or system that is requesting access to another person, resource, or system.

Authenticity: The ability to know that the information accessed is genuine. Authenticity controls include transaction confirmation, product validation, and range checking.

Availability: The accessibility and usability of information.

Best practices: A set of METASeS recommendations, gleaned from actual industry experience with hundreds of clients and consulting projects, for bringing an organization's Information Security up to world-class levels.

Business to Business (B2B): Systems that enable enterprises to conduct business with each other by extending the traditional business process and support systems beyond the company borders. Business to Government (B2G) systems share similar characteristics.

Business to Consumer (B2C): Applications that enable customers to transact business over the Internet with organizations, and vice-versa.

Confidentiality: The goal of keeping information private.

Consumer to Consumer (C2C): Systems providing a cyber place that enables end customers to transact business directly with other customers.

Cracker: Someone who illicitly and electronically tries to break into a system. Technically, a "hacker" can refer to someone who is authorized to break into a system, often to test the system's vulnerabilities.

Demilitarized Zone (DMZ): The DMZ configuration isolates network elements such as e-mail servers that, because they can be accessed from trustless networks, are exposed to external attacks.

Denial of Service (DoS): Attacks characterized by sufficiently large numbers of requests to a Web site to suspend operations.

Deployment/implementation: The deployment/implementation phase of the System Development Life Cycle (SDLC) puts the system into operation.

Development: The development phase of the System Development Life Cycle (SDLC) involves the coding of the system, and reflects the requirements and design decisions.

Directory: A repository of related information such as a list of telephone numbers. Directory services provide a mechanism for accessing information within the directory.

Disintermediation: The effect of Internet services in cutting out the middleman, that is, brokers, retailers, agents, and sales personnel.

Domain Name System (DNS): A convention that maps the names of objects, usually host names, to IP addresses or other resource record values.

Encryption: The scrambling of sensitive information to render it unintelligible to all but the intended recipient.

Enterprise-Wide Information Security Program Model: Defines and describes the high-level functions and components of an Information Security program. It provides the framework to develop, implement, and maintain integrated Information Security solutions that match risk management objectives. The elements of the Model are Framework, Organization, Technology, and Process.

"Ethical hacking": Illicit entry into an organization or system by a legitimate party in order to determine vulnerabilities.

Fail-over: Methods for lessening the impact of service failures or interruptions.

Firewall: A hardware platform combined with specialized software or firmware that protects the resources of a private network from users on other networks.

FTP: File Transfer Protocol (FTP).

Gap analysis: The difference or gap between the current state and the desired future state of security.

Hacker: See cracker.

HTTP: Hyper Text Transfer Protocol.

Information risk management: The identification, assessment, and appropriate mitigation of vulnerabilities and threats that can adversely impact the organization's information or data assets.

Information Security Charter: The authoritative mission statement for the Information Security Policy Framework that establishes how to support critical business objectives. The charter outlines key program management issues, such as policy enforcement and management responsibilities.

Information Security Policy Framework: The hierarchy of security policies, standards, and procedures. Provides the overall foundation for an effective Information Security program. The METASeS Information Security Policy Framework provides a best practice model to assess your current Information Security polices, and performs a gap analysis against its best practice reference model to highlight necessary improvements. It also provides a baseline reference model that you could customize to address your organization's unique needs – based on its business requirements, culture, industry regulations, etc.

Integrity: The consistency of the data. It specifically relates to the need to ensure that an unauthorized person or system cannot inadvertently or intentionally alter data without the modification being detected.

Intranet: Traditional, internal company Web sites supporting information sharing among and across various business functions. Examples include human resources (benefits elections, employee phone book, etc.), finance (financial submission and reporting), engineering and design (project management, distributed design, etc.), and marketing and sales.

Intrusion Detection System (IDS): A security application that detects anomalies that may indicate malicious activity on a network or network device.

Mail servers: A communications hub and telephone directory for routing electronic messages from user to user over networks and the Internet. Mail servers are typically dedicated computers used to store and forward electronic messages to users who can receive messages through an enabled mail client.

Maintenance/operations: The maintenance/operations phase of the System Development Life Cycle (SDLC) is the long-term activity of implementing program fixes and upgrades.

Non-repudiation: The ability to ensure that parties in a transaction cannot deny (repudiate) that the transaction took place.

Policy: The broad rules for ensuring the protection of information assets, and for implementing a security program. Generally brief in length, policies are independent of particular technologies and specific solutions.

Policy area: The categories of the Information Security (InfoSec) Policy Framework, namely: Asset Identification and Classification, Asset Protection, Asset Management, Acceptable Use, Vulnerability Assessment and Management, and Threat Assessment and Management.

Policy interpretation: The application of existing policy guidance to a new IT or Information Security topic. Good policy interpretation adopts new technology without having to make wholesale changes or additions to existing policy.

Policy life cycle: A series of phases that make up policy development, implementation, and maintenance.

POP3: Post Office Protocol version 3.

Possession: The treatment of data that a user owns but is not necessarily aware of.

Program: The complete, overarching set of items that address Information Security risk.

Process: Longer-term security program elements, such as risk assessment and security architecture development, that might take days or weeks, or are ongoing in nature.

Procedures: Specific, step-by-step advice on how to implement the various standards. They are shorter-term security program elements that typically last minutes, hours, or days. An NT configuration procedure would define, in detail, how to configure NT passwords.

Public Web site: Traditional, organization Web sites for information dissemination. Examples include organizational home pages, news and press releases, product/service descriptions, employment opportunities, and contact information.

Remote access servers: Servers that allow remote users to connect to organizational computing resources such as internal mail and data servers.

Requirements: The requirements phase of the System Development Life Cycle (SDLC) defines the software project, and outlines the parameters required for its accomplishment.

Risk construct: An illustration that illustrates the layers of threats faced by an organization.

Risk formula: An equation in which Risk is equal to Threats multiplied by Vulnerabilities multiplied by Asset Value.

Routers: The basic network devices used to interconnect networks.

Software change control: The process of managing and controlling changes that are requested after the approval of the system requirements document. It is a structured maintenance mechanism that tracks software modifications and controls version releases to enable a systematic, managed distribution.

SNMP: Simple Network Management Protocol.

Software Quality Assurance (SQA): A program of action for prevention, early detection, and efficient removal or modification of defects from software products.

Standard: The acceptable level of security for a specific policy area. Standards may be technology- or solution-specific, and provide more measurable criteria for satisfying the high-level objectives defined in the policies. An operating system standard may state the requirements for hardening the operating system to provide adequate security.

System Development Life Cycle (SDLC): The standard phases of system development, namely: Requirements, Architecture and Design, Development, Testing, Deployment/Implementation, and Maintenance/Operations.

System-level architecture: An architecture involving a subnetwork or a specific business system, and including a more specific set of goals and requirements that drive the system design.

Testing: The testing phase of the System Development Life Cycle (SDLC) attempts to identify functional and run-time problems that may impact system functionality.

TFTP: Trivial File Transfer Protocol.

Threats: Crackers or others who could try to break into your network – from without or within – and compromise your data. They also include people or things that may purposefully, inadvertently, or accidentally harm assets. Internal employees, for example, may accidentally damage or destroy valuable information. Note that a threat, strictly speaking, is a person or persons, not a thing or condition.

Traceability: The connections between top-level policy, other security framework components, and the business and mission goals they support.

Utility: The usefulness of information. For example, if the encryption key to data were erased by accident, the usefulness of the information would be lost.

Virtual Private Network (VPN): A network that is distributed across public networks, yet provides integrity, confidentiality, and in many cases authenticity of the data transmitted across public lines, thus making the distributed network seem private. VPNs are essentially encrypted network connections that allow computers to transmit data across the Internet or some other public network.

VPN (Virtual Private Network) gateways: The end points of a VPN. A VPN gateway is essentially a secure router that communicates with the destination network.

Vulnerabilities: The holes or weaknesses in information systems and procedures that intruders can exploit.

Vulnerability assessment: Identifies and prioritizes an organization's technical, organizational, procedural, administrative, or physical security weaknesses.

Web servers: Standard Internet devices that offer interactive services to customers and affiliates.

Index

Tell Us What You Think

As a reader, you are the most important critic of and commentator on our publications. We value your opinion and want to know what we're doing right, what we can do better, what areas you'd like to see us publish in, and any other words of wisdom you're willing to pass our way. You can help us make strong publications that meet your needs and give you the Information Security guidelines and standards you require.

DefenseONE-CommandCenter.com welcomes your comments. You can fax, email or write to us directly to let us know what you did or didn't like about this publication.

Here's the information:

METASeS
Attn: DefenseONE-CommandCenter.com
20464-A Chartwell Center Drive
Cornelius, North Carolina 28031
(704) 895-0837 Main number
email: DefenseONE-CommandCenter.com@metagroup.com

About METASeS™

Founded in January 1999, META Secur e-COM Solutions (METASeS) is an independent Internet security professional services firm employing an elite team of Internet security experts to provide a Web-based, quality-first approach to securing a company's cyberspace. In addition to providing high-end, on-site consulting services, METASeS provides comprehensive security services and solutions over the Internet – making it the first security company to offer this level of service and value over this highly effective medium.

About
DefenseONE-Command Center.com™

Because business, technology, and security are all moving and changing at light speed, you need an efficient and cost-effective way to keep your security program up-to-date. With DefenseONE-CommandCenter.com (DefenseONE-CommandCenter.com@metagroup.com) you now have access to an elite corps of security experts that provides you with valuable support and publications at a fraction of the cost associated with traditional consulting services. While other consultants provide only "snapshot" solutions, DefenseONE-CommandCenter.com addresses your ongoing security concerns by keeping our best practice publications up-to-date. Customers can purchase individual publications from our portfolio. Organizations that sign up with the DefenseONE-CommandCenter.com subscription service receive regular publication updates and the timely information required to maintain a top-notch security program.

For more information on the DefenseONE-CommandCenter.com subscription service, call 1-877-908-META.